CONTENTS

FOREWORD

> **It was the first time I was allowed to stay up to see in the New Year. I was seven, there were visitors coming and after supper we were to play cards.**

My repertoire of card games was Snap, Old Maid and Beggar-My-Neighbour – games where cards are played in turn – but that night I learned Racing Demon, a game which breaks all the rules about waiting for your turn and where fortune favours the speediest player. By midnight I had mastered the game, was trouncing the grown-ups and was rather put out when play stopped for 'Auld Lang Syne'.

Card playing is a fantastic way to spend time with friends and family. If you've never played Cheat you'll be amazed at how brilliantly the most angelic child can tell a bare-faced lie, yet grown-ups get rumbled straight away. Cards are also perfect for playing with people you hardly know. After one evening in dull company, Samuel 'Dictionary' Johnson remarked, 'I am sorry

I have not learnt to play at cards. It is very useful in life.' He was quite right then, and even today every county in England still has at least one pub where you can have a game of Cribbage over which you're sure to strike up a conversation with a stranger.

Until now there have been two sorts of books on card games. *The Complete Gamester* of 1674 explained how to play all the card games then known. And Edmond Hoyle's *Treatise on Whist* of 1742 was the first book about how to improve your card-play. Whist was very fashionable then, like Bridge is today, and readers studied Hoyle's book hoping to learn enough to avoid embarrassment at parties. There have been many more such encyclopaedia and self-improvement manuals since but it seems that David Parlett, the ingenious games inventor, has invented the first really new sort of book on card games since 1742.

You won't find complicated rules for Bridge or stodgy guidance to improve your Poker play but you will discover a carefully curated selection from the most popular types of card games. Cribbage, Racing Demon and Cheat are all here but if you haven't heard of half of the others, don't be surprised: many originate from far-away lands and some were invented by David Parlett himself. The games are organised according to common features in the rules rather than A to Z, so you can choose a game either for variety or for the familiarity it affords. A few words give a flavour of a game's history or geographical origin and explanations of how to play are kept very short and super-clear so that they can be read aloud and anyone can pick up the rudiments of how to play in a nanosecond.

David Parlett's books are much loved by people who enjoy trying new and different games, so it is with complete confidence that I commend this fine little volume to your hands in the firm belief that you will find it useful in life.

Edward Copisarow

INTRODUCTION

Cards have been popular for over 600 years because they offer so much variety and versatility. There are games for any number of players from one to seven – some for even more – and to suit every taste. Games can range from the childishly simple to the brain-bustingly complex. They can be played for fun, for money, for mental exercise, or for all these reasons at once.

After 50 years of studying (and inventing) card games I never cease to be amazed and delighted at all the things you can do with a simple pack of 52 cards marked with symbols, numbers and pictures of medieval characters. There are hundreds of recognizably different card games, and thousands if you take into account all their variations. Likewise hundreds, if not thousands, of compilations of card games have been and continue to be published in almost every language under the sun. So what's the point of yet another one?

New and Old Combined

As its title suggests, *Card Games* offers a selection of new and traditional games ideal for domestic recreation – easy to learn, fun to play and sufficiently varied to entertain a mix of players of all ages. For this purpose, it seemed best to skip games like Bridge and Poker that are played at tournament level with extreme seriousness and under strict control. Most card games are folk games, varying considerably from place to place, and remaining free from 'official rules'. If you don't like any of the 'rules' given here,

just change them. No one will mind, so long as you keep it in the family and everyone who's playing by them agrees on what they are. I also exclude gambling games of the sort played in physical and online casinos, except in the simplest form playable with counters, matchsticks or paperclips, such as Pontoon.

How the Games Are Grouped

The games are arranged in sections according to their similarities: card-catching and counting games; shedding games; matching games; trick-taking games; and one-player games. The chances are, if you find a game you especially enjoy, you will probably like others of the same type. Not everybody, for example, likes trick-taking games, and some will prefer games that don't involve mental arithmetic.

The Games

This is a list of the games that are included, together with the number of players required for each game to help you choose the most suitable one for your situation.

Card-Catching and Counting Games

Shedding Games

Matching Games

Trick-Taking Games

One-Player Games

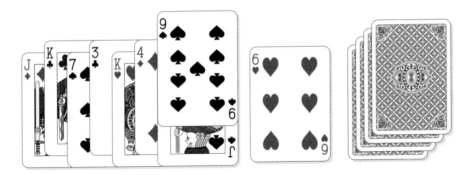

All categories also include a few games of my own invention that I hope you'll enjoy. They include Abstrac, Black Hole, Brummy, Centurion, Collusion, Dracula, Memoranda, Parity and Slapstick.

David Parlett, London
www.parlettgames.uk

THE BASICS

While there is a huge variety of games that can be played with a standard deck of cards, you will encounter the following every time you play.

❖ **Suits:** The standard pack or deck contains 52 cards divided into four series or 'suits' of 13 cards each. Each suit is distinguished by a black or red symbol. All suits are equal, but some games may attach more importance to one than to another, or arrange them in an order of importance.

❖ **Ranks:** The individual members of each suit, its 13 'ranks', are basically the numerals 1 to 10, plus three face cards – King, Queen and Jack (formerly Knave). The numeral 1 is called Ace. In trick-taking games, and some others, it is not the lowest but the highest card, outranking even the King. In a few games Ace counts either high or low, as you prefer.

❖ **Jokers:** The pack normally includes from one to three Jokers, but these are only used in a few games. Typically, they are used as 'wild' cards, meaning that each one can represent any card you like.

❖ **Shuffle, Cut and Deal:** The whole point of playing-cards is that each one is only identifiable from its front. So you normally start a game by shuffling the pack and dealing them face down to the players. You then pick them up and hold them in such a way that you can only identify your own cards and can't tell (yet) who holds what. Shuffling cards comes naturally to some people, but always improves with practice. It's usually best to let the best shuffler do the hard work, but it's a common rule that the dealer is entitled to shuffle last.

Before dealing, you should offer the deal to your right-hand neighbour to perform the cut, the purpose of which is to prevent the bottom card from being seen. You cut the cards by lifting approximately half of them in a packet from the top, placing the packet face down on the table, and putting the other half on top of it.

A game normally consists of a number of deals, with each person dealing in turn. The turn to play usually passes to the left, that is, clockwise as viewed from above. You deal cards one by one (unless the rules say otherwise) from the top, starting with the player on your left and finishing with yourself. A final note on card-playing etiquette: it's considered impolite to pick up your hand of cards until they have all been dealt.

Card-catching games, like Snap! and Beggar-My-Neighbour, are mostly simple games – ideal for children and beginners – where your aim is to capture the whole pack, or as many cards as possible. Equally simple, for the most part, are counting games, in which cards count only for their numbers and suits play little or no part. These range from the straightforward adding up of Twenty-Nine to the more complicated contortions of mental arithmetic demanded by Twenty-Four and Centurion.

CATCHING & COUNTING GAMES

SNAP!

This may be a simple game for children, but it undoubtedly requires skill in making snap decisions. A good start for budding tycoons.

Below: *Snap it first and you win the whole pile!*

❖ **Players**: Two to seven.

❖ **Cards**: 52.

❖ **Deal**: Deal all the cards round one at a time. It doesn't matter if some have one more than others. Hold your cards face down in a stack, or lay them face down in a pile in front of you.

✣ **Object:** To win all the cards.

✣ **Play:** You each in turn play the top one of your cards face up to a pile in the middle. If the card you play matches the previous card (King on King, Three on Three, and so on), whoever first calls 'Snap!' wins the central pile and places it face down at the bottom of their pile.

✣ **Ties:** If two players snap simultaneously, the central pile is placed to one side as a pool (or on top of one if it already exists) and a new pile is started. Whenever a card played to the main pile matches the top card of the pool, the pool is won by the first player to call 'Snap pool!'

✣ **Mistakes:** If anyone snaps mistakenly, the central pile is added to the pool.

✣ **Winning:** A player who runs out of cards drops out of play. The winner is whoever wins all the cards.

BEGGAR-MY-NEIGHBOUR

Also called Beat Your Neighbour Out of Doors, or Pay Me.

❖ **Players:** Two to seven.

❖ **Cards:** 52.

❖ **Deal:** Deal all the cards out in ones. It doesn't matter if some have one more than others. Hold your cards face down in a stack, without looking at them.

❖ **Object:** To win all the cards.

❖ **Play:** At each turn, you play your top card face up to a central pile. If you play one of the four highest ('pay-me') cards, the next in turn must then play immediately to the top of the pile:

Annie

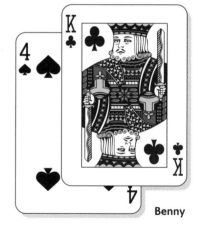

Benny

Above: *Annie's fourth card is a Queen so Benny must pay her two cards. But the second of these is a King, so Connie must pay one. But that one is a Jack, so Denny must pay her one card. As the 9♣ isn't a pay-me card, Connie wins them all.*

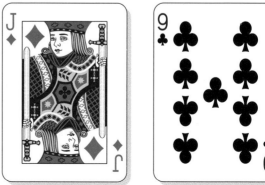

Connie

Denny

- one card for a Jack

- two cards for a Queen

- three cards for a King

- four cards for an Ace

If all the cards played on a pay-me card are numerals, you win the central pile of cards and add them to bottom of your own pile. But if one of them is a pay-me card, then the next in turn must pay the appropriate number of cards.

❖ **Winning:** You win by capturing all 52 cards.

SLAPJACK

Like Snap!, this is another game that's best played at great speed.

✤ **Players:** Two to seven.

✤ **Deal:** Deal all the cards round in ones. Stack your cards face down in a neat pile on the table in front of you.

✤ **Object:** To win cards by being the first to slap a Jack when one turns up.

✤ **Play:** You each in turn play the top card from your pile face up to a pile on the table. That pile is won by the first player to slap their hand on it when a Jack appears. Upon winning a pile, you shuffle it in with your existing cards and start a new round.

Above: *The first player to slap the Jack wins the cards.*

Mistakes: If you slap a card that isn't a Jack, you must forfeit one card to whoever played the card you slapped.

Running out: If you run out of cards, you can still keep playing by being the first to slap a Jack whenever one appears.

Winning: You win the game by winning all the cards. Or, if nobody else has the stamina to go any further, by having the most cards when they give up.

STUMP

A cross between Beggar-My Neighbour and Slapjack.

Players: Two to seven.

Cards: 52.

Deal: Deal all the cards out face down. It doesn't matter if some have one more than others. Hold your cards face down in a stack, without looking at them.

Object: To win all the cards.

Play: Play as Beggar-My-Neighbour but with this addition: if the card played to the top of the pile is a duplicate of a number from 2 to 10 that has already been played, the pile is won by whoever first slaps the top (duplicate) card.

Winning: You win by capturing all 52 cards.

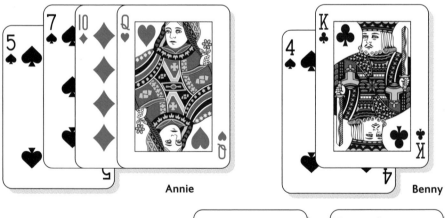

Annie   Benny

Left: *Like Beggar my Neighbour, but this time Denny plays a card matching a previous numeral (10). Whoever slaps it first wins them all.*

Connie   Denny

BATTLE!

One of the oldest games known.

❖ **Players**: Two to seven.

❖ **Cards**: 52.

❖ **Deal**: Deal all the cards round in ones. It doesn't matter if some have one more than others. Hold your cards face down in a stack, or lay them face down in a pile in front of you.

❖ **Object**: To win all the cards.

❖ **Play**: At each turn you play your top card face up to the table. Whoever plays the highest card, regardless of suit, wins all the cards played in that round, or trick, and places them at the bottom of their pile. If tied, those cards are won by whoever wins the next untied round.

❖ **Winning**: A player who runs out of cards drops out of play. The winner is whoever wins all the cards.

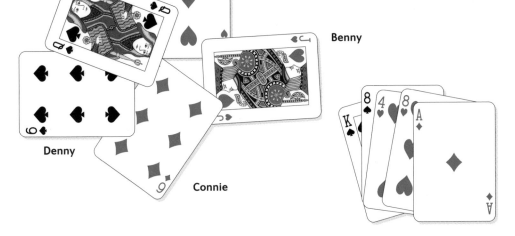

Above: *The previous round was tied because two players played an Eight. Now Annie leads with 3♥, and then Ernie beats them all with his Queen, winning these and the five cards played previously.*

MEMORY

This game used to be called Pelmanism, but nowadays only Google remembers who Pelman was.

* **Players:** Two to seven.

* **Cards:** 52

* **Deal:** None! Just shuffle the cards and scatter them face down all over the table.

* **Object:** To win cards by matching them up in pairs (two Kings, two Fives, or whatever).

* **Play:** You each in turn pick up two cards and look at them secretly. If they match you win the pair. If not, you replace them in exactly the same positions without revealing them.

✛ **Winning**: The player with most pairs wins.

✛ **Optional rules**:

- Upon winning a pair you play again.

- You may agree that if you don't get a pair you must show everyone the cards you turned up.

Above: *This player has found a pair of Eights!*

MEMORANDA

A more elaborate memory game.

- **Players:** Three to five.

- **Cards:** Two 52-card packs with different back designs or colours so they don't get mixed up.

- **Deal:** A game consists of as many deals as there are people playing. Players take it in turn to deal. The dealer shuffles one pack and deals them all out evenly amongst the other players.

- **Start:** You each take your hand of cards and try to memorize them. Meanwhile, the dealer shuffles the other pack and keeps an eye on the clock. After an agreed period of time (say 30 seconds) the dealer says 'Time's up.' Everyone then lays their hand of cards face down in a pile in front of themselves.

- **Play:** The dealer turns cards face up one by one from the second pack, announces what each one is, and lays it face up on the table before him or her. Anyone who thinks such a card is one they memorized says 'Mine!' and takes it. If nobody claims it, the dealer waits a second or two and then turns the next, after which the unclaimed card can no longer be called for. If more than one person claims a card, the dealer adds it face up to a separate pile of duplicate claims.

- **Scoring:** When the last card has been turned and either claimed or not, you each compare your original hand of cards with those you have claimed and score as follows:
  - For each perfect match, 1 point.
  - For a non-match (a wrongly claimed card), minus 1 point.
  - For a card matching one in the pile of duplicated claims, 2 points.

- **Game:** Scores are carried forward to the next deal and the winner is the player with the highest total when everybody has dealt once.

❖ **Optional extras**: If there are only three to four players, you may want to reduce both packs to 40 cards by removing numerals 2, 3 and 4. You may also want to use a stopwatch to ensure a consistent memorizing period.

No Claims

Duplicate

Above: *Dealer has just turned 9♥ from the second pack. If no one claims it, it will be added to the No Claims pile; if more than one player claims it, it will go on the Duplicate pile.*

GOPS

Some say that the name is an acronym for 'Game of Pure Strategy'. Maybe so, but some children just seem to win by instinct.

❖ **Players:** Usually two, playable by three.

❖ **Cards:** 52.

❖ **Deal:** Remove all the Diamonds, shuffle them, and lay them face down as a draw pile. Give each player all 13 cards of one other suit. If only two play, the remaining suit is ignored.

❖ **Object:** To win the greatest value of Diamonds, counting Ace as 1, numerals at face value, Jack as 11, Queen as 12, King as 13.

❖ **Play:** At each 'trick', the top Diamond is turned face up. The players then bid for it by choosing any card from their hand and laying it face down on the

table. When all are ready, the bid-cards are turned face up. Whoever plays the highest card (Ace low, King high) wins the Diamond. The bid-cards are put aside, and the next trick played in the same way.

❖ **Ties:** If two both bid the same amount, their bids are discarded and the current Diamond is won by the winner of the next Diamond. If the last card or cards are tied, they belong to no one. If two tie for best when three play, the Diamond is won by the third player. A three-way tie is won by no one.

❖ **Winning:** The winner is the player who captures the greatest face value of Diamonds. As the maximum possible is 91, the target for two players is 46, for three, 31.

Below: Yvonne wins the **8♦**, but she could have got it much more cheaply and gone forwards with greater purchasing power.

Yvonne

Zandy

SCOPA

Like most Italian games this one is played with 40 cards, and all play passes to the right around the table.

❖ **Players**: Two or three.

❖ **Cards**: 40, made by stripping out all numerals 8, 9, 10.

❖ **Object**: To win cards.

❖ **Deal**: Deal three cards each in ones face down, four to the table face up, and set the remainder aside as a stock. When everyone has played their three cards, deal three more each from the stock. Continue until all cards have been won.

❖ **Play**: You each in turn play a card from your hand and try to capture one or more table cards with it. Cards can be captured by either:

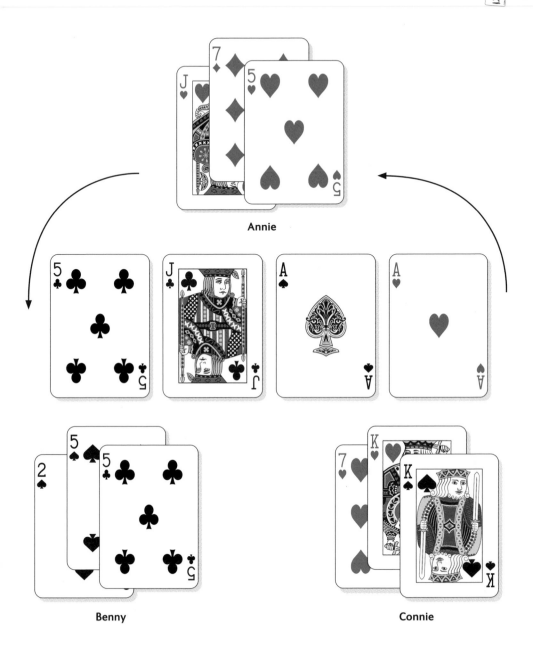

Annie

Benny   Connie

Above: *Annie, to start, would love to use her sette bello (7♦) to capture 5+1+1 by summing, but is obliged to capture the J♣ with her J♥. Benny, next, can't pair anything but can capture both Aces with his 2♠. That counts as a sweep, so he places one of his cards face up on his winnings pile. Connie, with nothing left to capture, can only trail. She adds a King to the table, hoping to pair it with her other King next time round. Annie trails her 5♥, and Benny forestalls Connie by taking the King she had to put down.*

- **Pairing:** An Ace takes an Ace, a Two a Two, and so on. Only one card may be paired in one turn, and you must make a pair if you can; **or**

- **Summing**: If you can't pair, your card can take two or more table cards totalling the same as itself, counting numerals at face value (1 to 7), Jack as 8, Queen as 9, King as 10. Thus a Seven will capture two or more cards totalling 7 (A+6, 2+2+3, etc), a Jack two or more totalling 8, and so on. You can only make one summing capture at a time.

Having captured, you place both the captured and the capturing cards face down in front of you and end your turn. If you capture all the cards on the table, leaving none for the next player to take, it is a *scopa* or 'sweep'. You indicate this by leaving the capturing card face up in front of you and will eventually score 1 point for it.

- **Trailing:** If you can't make any capture, you must 'trail' by playing any card face up to the table with those already there (if any).

- **Ending:** When no stock cards remain, whoever made the last capture wins all the other table cards with it. This doesn't count as a sweep, even if it technically is one.

- **Scoring:** You then sort through their won cards and score points as follows:

- 1 for taking the most cards. If tied, no one scores.

- 1 for having captured **7♦** , or *sette bello*.

- 1 for taking the most Diamonds. If tied, no one scores.

- 1 for *primiera* (see below).

- 1 per sweep, as indicated by face-up cards.

For *primiera*, you each take the highest card you captured in each suit and add their special values together. Only each player extracts the highest-scoring card they have in each of the four suits, and the player whose four have the highest combined value scores the point. If a player took only three suits they can't compete. For this purpose only, cards count as follows: Seven 21, Six 18, Ace 16, Five 15, Four 14, Three 13, Two 12, face cards 10 each.

- **Game:** The game ends when a player reaches 11 or more points, and the winner is the person who has scored most.

TWENTY-NINE

Twenty-Nine, in one form or another, is widely played throughout South Asia, especially India. The full-blown versions are too wordy to describe here, but the following is relatively simple.

Below: A seven-card trick.

💠 **Players:** Two to six.

💠 **Cards:** 52, but for three, five or six players, remove as many Tens as necessary for everyone to receive the same number of cards.

💠 **Card values:** Aces and face cards count as 1 each, numerals at face value.

💠 **Object:** To win the most cards in tricks.

💠 **Deal:** Deal all the cards around in ones.

Play: The dealer's left-hand neighbour plays any card face up to the table and announces its face value. Each in turn contributes a card to the count and announces the new total. The count may not exceed 29. If you can't play without exceeding 29, you miss a turn. Whoever makes it exactly 29 wins the cards so far played and turns them face down like a won trick. The next trick is started by the player to the left of the previous trick-winner.

Winning: The last trick may total less than 29; if so, it belongs to whoever played last. The winner is the player who has won the most cards.

NINETY-NINE

Said to be a travellers' game.

❖ **Players:** Three to six.

❖ **Cards:** 52.

❖ **Card values and powers:**
- Ace   1 or 11
- K, Q, J   10 each
- 10   plus or minus 10
- 9   brings the count to exactly 99
- others   at face value except
- 4   0, but changes the direction of play

❖ **Deal:** Deal three cards each in ones and stack the rest face down. Play goes to the left initially (clockwise), but may change.

❖ **Play:** You each in turn play a card face up to the table, announce the total face value of all cards so far played, and draw a replacement from the stock. The count may not exceed ninety-nine. If you can't play without exceeding 99, you lose a life.

❖ **Ending:** The first to lose three lives is the overall loser.

Draw

Below: *Annie starts. Later, her* **4♠** *adds 0 and changes direction to anti-clockwise, so Denny plays next. Benny's* **4♥** *changes it back to clockwise and now Connie continues. Annie's* **9♣** *makes 99, so Benny, who is next to play, loses – unless he has a 10, which will bring it back down to 89.*

Annie

Benny

Connie

Denny

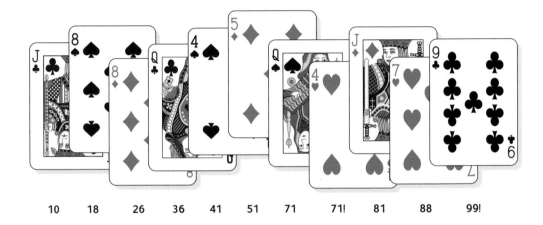

10   18   26   36   41   51   71   71!   81   88   99!

HUNDRED

One of many arithmetical games popular in central European countries.

❖ **Players:** Two to six.

❖ **Cards:** 32, omitting all cards lower than 7. Their counting values are:

A	K	Q	J	10	9	8	7
11	4	3	2	10	9	8	7

❖ **Object:** To bring the counting value of cards played to exactly 100.

❖ **Deal:** Divide cards equally amongst the players, leaving any left over face up on the table to start the count.

❖ **Play:** Each in turn, starting with the dealer's left-hand neighbour, plays one card to the table, adds its value to the previous count, and announces the new one. If you make it over 100 you lose, but for making it 100 exactly you win. You may agree to continue play with another scoring point at 200.

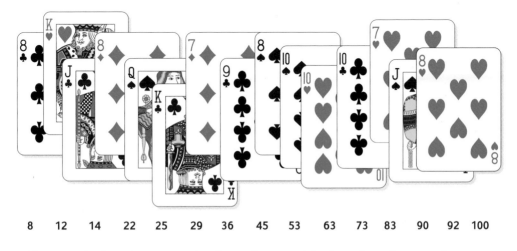

| 8 | 12 | 14 | 22 | 25 | 29 | 36 | 45 | 53 | 63 | 73 | 83 | 90 | 92 | 100 |

Above: *In this four-player game the player who started third won by making exactly 100 with J♠ .*

SCROOT

This simple game is based on one in an anonymously authored booklet produced years ago by the maths department of the (now defunct) Bourne School in Berkhamstead.

- **Players:** Two to seven.

- **Cards:** 52. Numerals count at face value, face cards count 1 each.

- **Deal:** Deal five cards each and stack the rest face down.

- **Object:** To produce square numbers (1, 4, 9, 16, 25, 36, 49, 64, 81, 100, 121, 144, 169, 196).

- **Play:** You each in turn play a card face up to a row on the table, announcing their total face value as you go along. If you make a square number you score its square root (e.g. if you make 81 you score 9). After each turn you take the top card of the stock.

- **Ending:** Play ends when the total exceeds 196. The highest score wins.

Annie   Benny

Connie   Denny

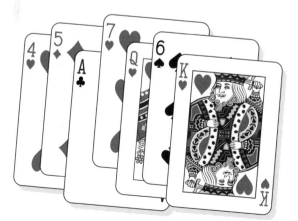

Above: Annie starts with 4, scoring 2; Benny adds 5, making 9 and scoring 3 for its square root. When the turn comes round to Connie again she can use her King to duplicate the previous 6, making 25 and scoring 5 for it.

4, 9, 10, 17, 18, 24, 25...

TWENTY-FOUR

This game is said to have originated in China but has since become widespread. There are many different variations and alternative rules.

✤ **Players**: Two, but see below for three and four.

✤ **Cards**: 40, omitting all 12 face cards. Numerals count at face value, upwards from Ace = 1.

✤ **Deal**: 20 each. Hold your stack face down without examining them.

✤ **Object**: At each turn, to make a total of 24 by combining the four cards on display using plus, minus, multiply and/or divide.

✤ **Play**: At each turn you put down the two top cards of your stack simultaneously. As soon as you can think of a way of making 24 out of them, you slap the cards and announce your calculation. For example, from 3, 5, 5 and 8, you can make (3x8)x(5÷5). If correct, your opponent adds the four cards to the bottom of their stack; if not, you add them to the bottom of yours. If neither of you has an answer, you each take back your two cards and place them at the bottom of your stack.

✤ **Winning**: The winner is the first player to get rid of all their cards.

✤ **For four players**: You each have a stack of 10 cards, and at each turn put one card out to make four in all. As soon as you can think of a calculation you slap the table but say nothing. When three players have slapped, the fourth chooses one of them to give their answer. If it's correct, the caller adds the cards to the bottom of their stack; if not, the incorrect player adds them to their own stack. You can, of course, bluff by slapping when you have no answer, in hope of not being chosen.

❖ **For three players:** As for four, but place the 10 unused cards face down in a stack. At each turn its top card is turned up to provide the fourth card.

❖ **Using 52 cards:** Some players include Jack = 11, Queen = 12 and King = 13. Or you can say that a face card can duplicate any of the numerals on display. For example, with 3, J, 5 and K, you could use one face card as 3 and the other as 5.

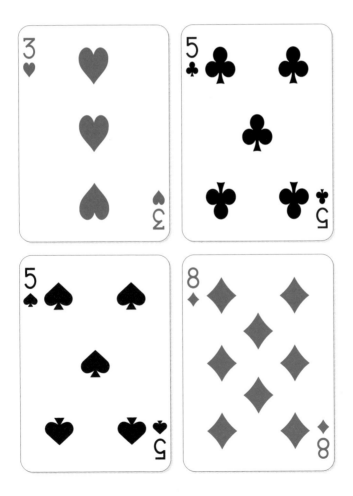

Above: *You can make 24 with (3 x 8) x (5 ÷ 5).*

CENTURION

A more complicated variation on adding up to 100.

- ❖ **Players**: Two.

- ❖ **Cards**: 52 and 1 to 4 optional Jokers.

- ❖ **Deal**: Deal seven cards each face down and stack the rest, also face down. Each card has a counting value, which is its face value multiplied by its suit value. The face values are Ace = 1, Two = 2, and so on up to Ten 10, Jack 11, Queen 12, King 13. The suit values are ♠ = 1, ♥ = 2, ♣ = 3, ♦ = 4. Thus the lowest card is **A♠** = 1 and the highest is **K♦** = 52. Jokers count as zero.

- ❖ **Object**: To bring the current value of all cards played to exactly 100, or, if overshot, by the next possible multiple of 10. (The shortest possible game consists of **K♦** and **Q♦**, i.e. 52 + 48.)

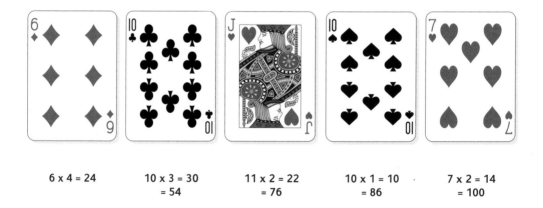

6 x 4 = 24	10 x 3 = 30	11 x 2 = 22	10 x 1 = 10	7 x 2 = 14
	= 54	= 76	= 86	= 100

Above: The first player (**6♦**)
reaches 100 on the fifth card (**7♥**).

Play: Starting with non-dealer, you each in turn play a card face up to the table and announce the accumulated total as you go along. Stop when it reaches exactly 100 or the next higher multiple of 10. If one of you runs out of cards the other continues playing alone. If both run out without hitting a target, deal seven more cards and continue play. When a target is reached, the next player may not add a Joker.

Hitting the target: Whoever hits a target takes and wins all the cards played.

End: The game ends when the only cards left in play will not reach 100. Whoever took the most cards wins.

DRACULA

This arithmetical game for two players (or partnerships) can be played for a small stake – preferably through the heart.

- **Players**: Two, but see below for four.

- **Cards**: 54, including two Vampires. (If there are no Vampires in your pack, use Jokers instead.)

- **Deal**: Decide who deals first by each cutting a card from the pack. The first dealer is the first player to cut a red suit, or the higher-ranking Heart if both are red. Before dealing, the first dealer announces whether he or she will score the Queen's way (horizontally) or the King's way (vertically), leaving no choice to the other. There are six deals to a game, each dealing in turn.

Deal four cards each, face down, turn the next one face up on the table, and stack the rest face down. Consider the face-up card as the centre of an eventual square of nine cards in three rows and three columns (as in Noughts & Crosses or Tic-Tac-Toe) which the players gradually build up on the table. This layout is called the coffin, and the initially face-up card is the first nail in the coffin.

- **Object**: To make the highest-scoring line of three cards in your scoring direction. For this purpose numerals count at face value from Ace = 1 to Ten = 10. Face cards count either 0 or 10 as explained below. The Queen-player scores only in the horizontal direction and the King-player only in the vertical direction.

- **Play.** Each in turn, starting with the non-dealer, plays a card face up to the table, edge to edge with a card already down. Keep going till all positions are full.

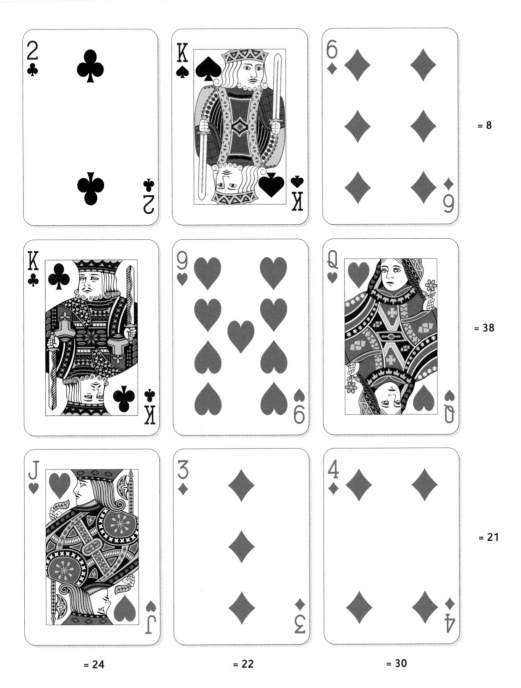

Above: *Yvonne, playing across, scores 38 for her middle row (9 + Q = 19, doubled for two hearts). Zandy's best column on the right counts 30, made by adding 6 and 4 and multiplying by three for three of the same colour. The Queen counts for nothing in Zandy's column, and the King for nothing in Yvonne's.*

❖ **Score:** You each score the total value of the highest-scoring line of cards in your own direction - across for one of you, down for the other. If both are equal, score your second-highest line, or, if still equal, your third-highest (even if equal). The score for any line of three is found by counting each numeral card at face value and face cards as follows:

- A Jack counts as 0 in either direction

- A Queen counts as 10 horizontally but 0 vertically

- A King counts as 10 vertically but 0 horizontally

Furthermore, the total face value of any line is:

- doubled if it contains two cards of the same suit

- trebled if it contains three of the same colour, or

- quintupled (x5) if it contains three of the same suit.

(The suit of a King, Queen or Jack that counts as zero still remains valid for doubling, trebling or quintupling the score of the line in which it appears.)

> **Remember**
> The value of individual cards is irrelevant here, it is the number of cards taken that counts.

A Vampire drains all the blood out of the row and column in which it appears, resulting in a whole line counting as zero in both directions.

❖ **Next deal:** The next dealer clears the coffin away, takes up the stock of unused cards, and deals four cards each face down and one face up as the first nail in the second coffin. Play and score as before.

❖ **Game:** The winner is the player with the highest total score after six deals.

❖ **Scoring with cards:** If you don't want to keep writing scores down, you can use cards as counters. When you make the highest-valued line, you take from the played cards one for each 10 in your score – that's one card if your winning line is from 10 to 19, two if 20 to 29, and so on up to a maximum of nine. Place these as won cards face down before you and discard the others to a waste pile. At the end of a game you can, if you wish, turn the waste pile down and use it to play one or more rounds, so long as at least nine cards remain.

Keep doing this until fewer than nine are left, then find your score by simply counting the number of cards you have won. If you follow this procedure you are not allowed to take a Vampire as a scoring card unless your best line scores 90 or more.

❖ **Dracula for Four Players:** Deal four hands of 13 cards each, and add a Vampire to the hand of the dealer's left-hand opponent and the dealer's partner. The dealer's left-hand opponent puts the first nail in the coffin, and all play passes to the left. Play and score as in the two-player game.

PONTOON

Pontoon is the domestic British version of an ancient, world-wide gambling game also known as Twenty-One and, in casinos, Blackjack. To save space, this is a simplified version.

❖ **Players**: Three to seven.

❖ **Cards**: 52. Numerals count at face value, face cards as 10 each, Ace as 1 or 11 as its player decides, according to circumstance.

❖ **Also needed**: Coins or counters, at least 20 each.

❖ **The banker**: Decide who banks first by dealing cards around face up till someone gets a Jack. The bank remains with that player till someone gets a pontoon, or, if so agreed, passes to the left after as many deals as there are players. Agree in advance what is the minimum and maximum initial stake.

❖ **Object**: To acquire a hand of cards whose total count exceeds the banker's but not over 21.

❖ **Pontoon**: A two-card hand totalling 21, necessarily consisting of an Ace and a 10 or face card, is a pontoon and wins double unless tied. A banker's pontoon is therefore unbeatable.

❖ **Deal**: Shuffle the cards thoroughly at start of play. They are not then shuffled before each deal but only after one in which a player gets a pontoon. Deal one card face down to each player and to the banker (last), then a second card face up to each player but face down to the banker.

❖ **Stakes**: The banker may not yet examine their hand, but everyone else examines their own hand and places a stake on them in accordance with the agreed minimum and maximum. Anyone dealt a pontoon must turn their Ace face up and may not stake any more in that deal.

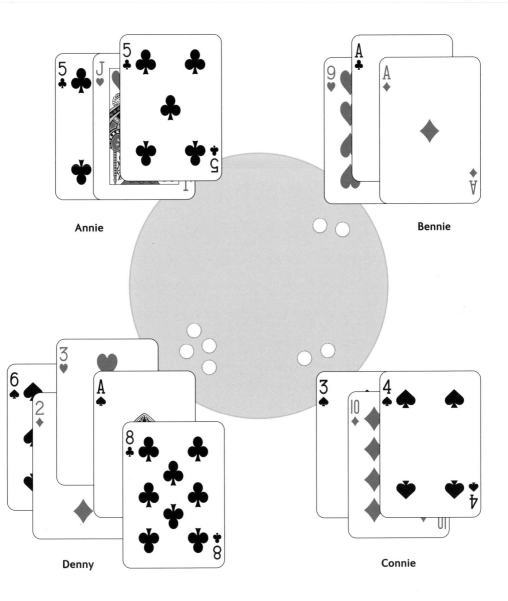

Above: *Everyone has paid an initial stake of one counter. Benny has 9 + A = 10 or 20 and buys one for one counter. His second Ace counts as 11, giving him 21. Connie has 13, buys one for one, and sticks at 17. Denny buys one for 2 counters and has 11. He buys another for 2 and now has 12 (not 22!). He 'twists' a free fifth card, which gives him 20 and a five-card trick. Banker Annie's 20 beats Connie's 17, but she must pay Benny 2 for his 21 and double Denny's 4 to 8 for his five-card trick.*

❖ **Splitting**: If you've been dealt two cards of the same rank you may choose to split them and play each one as a separate hand, turning them both up to show your entitlement to do so. The banker is not allowed this option.

❖ **More cards**: The banker then addresses each player in turn and asks whether they want more cards. These are your options when asked:

- **Stick:** This means you have a count of at least 16 and don't want any more cards.

- **Buy:** In this case, you increase your stake and are dealt another card face down. Your extra stake must be not less than your previous one, nor more than the total amount you have staked so far. If you reach a count of 11 or less on four cards you may not buy a fifth but may only twist.

- **Twist:** In this case, you are dealt one card face up, free of charge. Having twisted once, you may twist further cards but may not subsequently buy.

You continue buying or twisting till you bust, stick, or hold five cards without busting, when you must stick. If you bust, you lose your total stake and return your cards to the banker, who places them at the bottom of the pack.

When playing a split hand, you become two players (or more), and deal with each one separately before passing on to the next.

❖ **Showdown:** When everyone has been served, the banker's two cards are revealed and she or he may turn more cards face up till satisfied with the count, or is bust. If the banker gets:

- A pontoon, the player wins all the stakes.

- Twenty-one on three or more cards, the player pays double to anyone with a pontoon, but wins all the others' stakes.

- Under 21, the player pays anyone with a higher count (double for a pontoon) but wins all the other stakes.

- A bust, the player keeps the stakes of those who also bust, but pays anyone with a count of 16 to 21 (double for a pontoon).

- Pontoons. If you get a pontoon and the banker doesn't, you can take over as banker or sell that option to the highest bidder.

❖ **Optional extras:** The following optional extras may be included:

- Five-card trick. A five-card hand worth 21 or less beats everything except a banker's pontoon, and wins double.

- Royal pontoon. A hand consisting of three Sevens beats everything except a banker's pontoon, and is paid treble.

Your aim in these games is simply to be the first to get rid of all your cards. The usual method is that at each turn you play from your hand one or more cards that match the card or cards played out by the person before you. If you can't, you not only fail to shed any of your cards but also, more often than not, have to draw extra cards from a stockpile. But there are many interesting variations on this basic premise.

SHEDDING GAMES

NEWMARKET

Named after the famous horse-racing town and former centre of royalty, the play of Newmarket suggests racing to get through your cards first. In America, it's known as Michigan. Similar games are named after other racecourses.

❧ **Players.** Three to seven.

❧ **Cards.** 52, running 2 3 4 5 6 7 8 9 10 J Q K A.

❧ **Also needed:** A layout showing A♥ K♣ Q♦ K♠ ('boodle cards'), and chips or counters to use as stakes. The layout can be drawn on paper or card, or made using these cards from another pack.

❧ **Stakes:** Before dealing, the dealer places two chips and everybody else one chip on each of the boodle cards.

❧ **Deal:** The turn to deal passes to the left. Deal cards one at a time to each player and to a spare 'dead' hand till all are out. It doesn't matter if some players have one card more than others.

❧ **Object:** To win stakes placed on the boodle cards and to be the first to shed your hand of cards.

❧ **Start:** The dealer's left-hand neighbour starts by playing the lowest card held of any suit. Whoever holds the next higher card of that suit now plays it, likewise the holder of the next, and so on. Cards are placed face up in front of their players.

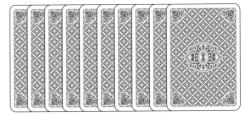

Below: Annie (A) starts off with **3** to **5♥**; Benny (B) plays the **6**, but the **7** is in the dead hand. So Benny starts a new run with his lowest Clubs. No one holds the **4**, so he continues now with Diamonds...

The dead hand

Boodle cards, with 2 chips from the dealer and one from each other player.

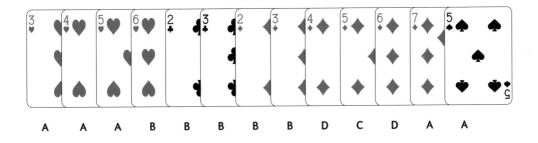

3♥	4♥	5♥	6♥	2♣	3♣	2♦	3♦	4♦	5♦	6♦	7♦	5♠
A	A	A	B	B	B	B	B	D	C	D	A	A

❖ **Stop and go:** Play continues till either an Ace is reached or no one can play the next higher card, either because it is in the dead hand or because it has already been played. Whoever played the last card (or 'stopper') starts a new race by playing the lowest card they hold of any desired suit.

❖ **Winning stakes:** Anyone who plays a card matching one of the boodle cards takes all the chips on that card.

❖ **Ending:** The game ends when somebody wins by playing their last card. Everyone pays the winner one chip for each card left in hand. Any chips left on the boodle cards are carried forward to the next deal.

PLAY OR PAY

A simpler relative of Newmarket.

⁜ **Players:** Three to seven.

⁜ **Cards:** 52, running 2 3 4 5 6 7 8 9 10 J Q K A.

⁜ **Deal:** Deal all the cards out as far as they will go.

⁜ **Object:** To be the first to shed your hand of cards.

⁜ **Play:** The dealer's left-hand neighbour plays any card face up to the table to start the race. Each in turn thereafter must either play the next highest card of the same suit or else pay a counter to a pool.

⁜ **Stop and go:** The race ends when it reaches an Ace, or any other card that can't be followed. Whoever played the last card starts a new one with any card.

⁜ **Winning:** First out of cards wins the pool, plus one chip for each card left in other players' hands.

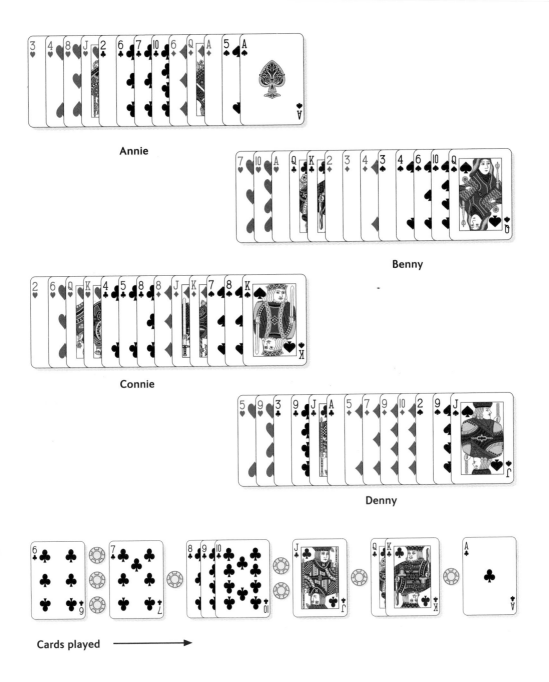

Annie

Benny

Connie

Denny

Cards played ⟶

Above: *Annie starts with* **6♣** *, knowing that the other three will each have to pay a counter to the pool before she continues with* **7♣** *. Benny pays a counter before Connie plays* **8♣** *. Later, when Denny plays* **Q♣** *and* **K♣** *he can start a new series with any card from his hand, probably* **5 ♦** *.*

SNIP-SNAP-SNORUM

Like so many good games for children, this goes back to an ancient drinking game.

❖ **Players:** Four to eight.

❖ **Cards:** 52, running A 2 3 4 5 6 7 8 9 10 J Q K.

❖ **Deal:** Deal all the cards out as far as they will go.

Connie	Connie	Annie	Denny	
Snip!	Snap!	Snorum!	High cockalorum!	Jingo!

Snip!	Snap!	Snorum!	
Benny	Benny	Denny	

Above: How the first two rounds might go.

+ **Object:** To be the first to shed your hand of cards.

+ **Play:** The dealer's left-hand neighbour plays any card face up to the table and calls 'Snip!' Whoever has the next higher card of the same suit plays it, saying 'Snap!' The player of the next card in sequence announces 'Snorum!', of the fourth 'High cockalorum!' and of the fifth 'Jingo'. The fifth card ends the run. Whoever played it starts a new one by playing any card and saying 'Snip!' Continue playing as above.

+ **Stop and go:** A run ends when the King is reached or the next required card has gone. Whoever ended it calls 'Jingo!' and starts a new one.

+ **Winning:** You win by being the first out of cards. Everyone else pays the winner one counter for each card remaining in their hand. (Or the winner scores that number of points.)

DOMINO

❖ **Players**: Two to seven. (The more the merrier.)

❖ **Cards**: 52, running A 2 3 4 5 6 7 8 9 10 J Q K.

❖ **Deal:** Deal all the cards out as far as they will go.

❖ **Object:** To be the first to shed your hand of cards.

❖ **Start:** The dealer's left-hand neighbour starts by playing any Seven face up to the table. If unable, they pay one counter to the pool and play passes to the next in turn.

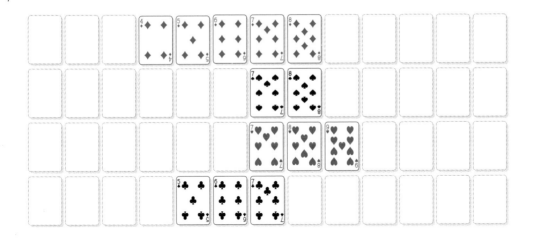

Above: *How the cards are built up into a layout, starting with **7♦**. You can play to the left or right of a card already down, and above or below it. You needn't spread the cards out like this: you can bunch them up, so long as all remain visible.*

Play: Once started, the next in turn must play either:

- the Six of the same suit to the left of the Seven, or

- the Eight of the same suit to its right, or

- any other Seven below it.

Thereafter, each in turn must play either a Seven, or the next higher or lower card of a suit-sequence, in such a way as to build up four rows of 13 cards, each of the same suit and running from Ace to King.

Pay: If unable to add a valid card to the layout contribute one counter to the pool. If you decline to play when able to do so, you pay three to each opponent, plus five to the holders of the Six and Eight of a suit if you hold the Seven and fail to play it. Not that you are obliged to do so: holding up Sevens is all part of the strategy.

Winning: First out sweeps the pool and gets one counter from each opponent for each card left in hand.

CRAZY EIGHTS

A very popular game with many different names and rules. This is the most basic version. The proprietary game of Uno is an elaboration of it.

❖ **Players**: Two to seven.

❖ **Cards**: 52, or 104 (two packs) for five or more.

❖ **Deal:** Five cards to each player (seven if only two play). Stack the rest face down as a draw pile and turn its top card face up to start a discard pile.

❖ **Object:** To be the first to shed your cards.

❖ **Play:** At each turn you either play a legal card face up to the discard pile, or draw the top card of the draw pile and add it to your hand. The following cards are legal:

- Any card of the same suit or rank. (For example, to **10♠** you can play another spade or any Ten.)

- Any Eight. In this case you nominate a suit for the next player to follow.

- If the top card is an Eight, any card of the suit nominated by whoever played it, or another Eight, after which you nominate a suit to be followed.

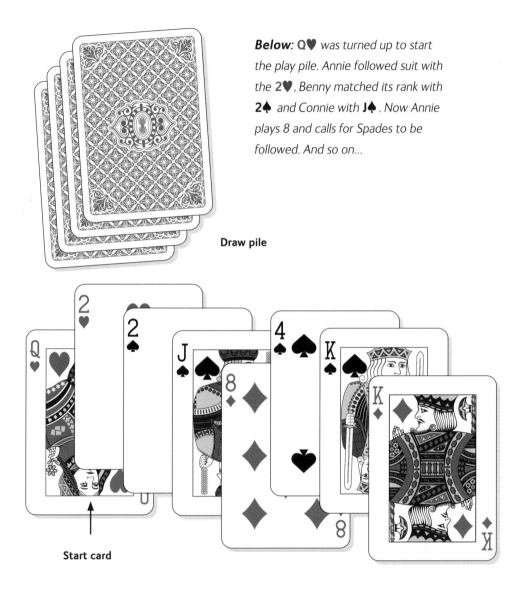

Draw pile

Below: **Q♥** *was turned up to start the play pile. Annie followed suit with the* **2♥**, *Benny matched its rank with* **2♠** *and Connie with* **J♠** *. Now Annie plays 8 and calls for Spades to be followed. And so on...*

Start card

❖ **Scoring:** The winner is the first out of cards. Everyone else scores penalty points for cards left in their hands, at the rate of 50 for an Eight, 10 for a face card, and numerals at face value (Ace = 1, Two = 2 and so on).

❖ **Renewing the draw pile:** When no cards remain in the draw pile the discard pile (except for its top card, which stays in place to start a new one) is picked up, shuffled, and turned face down to start a new one.

GO BOOM

A cross between Whist and Crazy Eights.

❖ **Players**: Three to six.

❖ **Cards**: 52, running 2 3 4 5 6 7 8 9 10 J Q K A.

❖ **Deal:** Deal eight each (or seven if five play, six if six).

❖ **Object:** To be the first to shed all your cards by playing them to tricks, which themselves have no value.

Draw pile

Below: At trick 1, Annie leads **K♥** and wins against the 5 and 3. She then leads **9♥**. Benny has no Hearts, but draws cards until – third time lucky – he gets **Q♥**, which wins the trick.

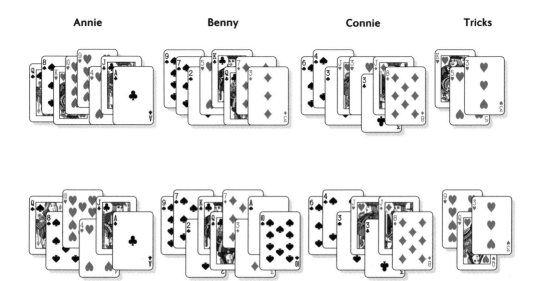

Annie	Benny	Connie	Tricks

Play: The dealer's left-hand neighbour leads to the first trick. The others must play a card of the same suit or rank as the card led. (For example, **Q♥** may be followed by any Hearts or Queen.) The player with the highest card turns the trick down and leads to the next. In the case of a draw, the player who went first wins the trick.

Drawing cards: If you can't play a required card you must draw cards from the stock and add them to your hand till you can. If you still can't follow when none remain, you just miss a turn.

Winning: The first to play the last card from their hand wins the game and scores, or is paid, according to the number of cards left in everyone else's.

SLAPSTICK

Hardly a game of skill, but it may keep you alert. It's like a game called Chicken Out! but without all the adding up.

✤ **Players:** Two to four.

✤ **Cards**: 52, plus as many Jokers as you like.

✤ **Deal:** Deal all cards out as far as they will go. Hold them face down in a pile and don't look at their faces.

✤ **Object:** To be the first to play out all your cards.

✤ **Start:** The dealer's left-hand neighbour starts by playing the top two cards of their hand face up to the table. If they are of the same rank, return them to the bottom of the hand and start again. (The same applies every time a new round is started.)

✤ **Play:** You each in turn play the top card of your hand face up to the table to form an overlapping row on the start cards. Continue until one of the following happens:

- You play a card matching the rank of either the first or last card in the row. Then the next player in turn must pick up the row of cards, add them to the bottom of their hand, and start a new row by playing two cards from the top.

- You play a card matching the rank of any other card in the row, or a Joker. You must pick up the row of cards, add them face down to the bottom of your own hand, and start a new row by playing two cards from the top.

- You chicken out (because you fear matching a middle card). You then pick up all the cards in the row, add them to the bottom of your hand, and start a new row by playing from the top as many cards as you like until you either make a match or run out of cards.

✤ **Winning:** The game ends when somebody wins by playing their last card.

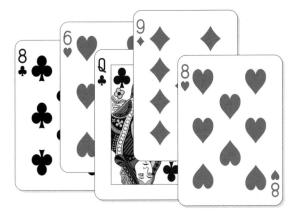

Four players:

Round 1: *Annie starts by turning an 8 and a 6. Denny's **8♥** matches the rank of the first card in the row. Annie must now add all these cards to the bottom of her hand and start a new row with two more cards.*

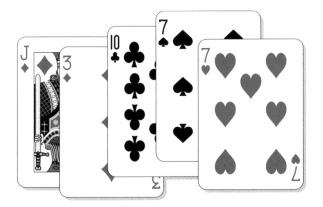

Round 2: *Annie turns a J and a 3. Denny matches the last card in the row, and lumbers Annie again.*

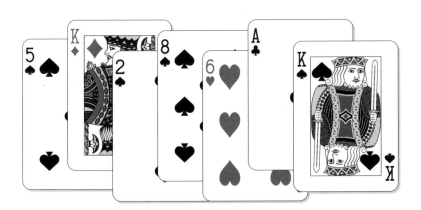

Round 3: *Benny's **K♠** matches an intermediate card, so he has to add them all to his hand and start a new row with two cards. He could instead have chickened out, picked them all up, and started a new row with as many cards as he liked, or dared.*

OLD MAID

A popular Victorian game, known in Germany as 'Black Peter' and in France as 'Old Boy', the odd card being a Jack.

❖ **Players:** Three to seven.

❖ **Cards:** 52, or 104 if more than five play, but with one Queen removed from the pack.

❖ **Deal:** Deal all the cards around as far as they will go. It doesn't matter if some players have one more card than others.

Below: Pass one to your left, receive one from your right. If it's a 7, 4, Q, 6 or 9, it makes a pair, which you then throw away.

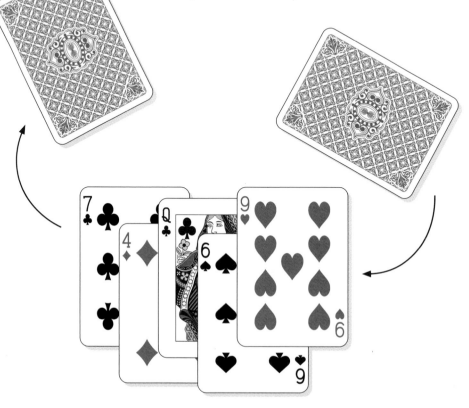

❖ **Object**: To shed all your cards, and especially avoid being left over with an unpaired Queen – the 'old maid' – in your hand.

❖ **Start**: You each examine your hand and discard, face down, any pairs of cards of the same rank (two Sevens, two Jacks and so on).

❖ **Play**: The dealer offers his or her hand of cards face down to their left-hand neighbour, who draws one and adds it to their hand. If this makes a pair, it is discarded. That player then offers their hand face down to their left neighbour, and the process is repeated. As players empty their hands by discarding pairs, they drop out of play.

❖ **Ending**: Eventually there will be only one player left, holding an unpaired Queen. That player is the loser, and pays a forfeit. Or, to delay the torture, the first player to lose three times pays the forfeit.

CUCKOO

This old European game, simple and fun, is also played in Britain as a gambling game under the name Chase the Ace or Ranter-Go-Round.

Players: Three to seven.

Cards: 52, running A 2 3 4 5 6 7 8 9 10 J Q K.

Deal: Players take turns to deal. Deal one card each.

CUCKOO!

Above: If your left-hand neighbour holds a King, they can refuse to give it up by showing it and saying 'Cuckoo!'.

<ul>
<li>Object: To avoid being left with the lowest card in hand.</li>

<li>Play: Each plays in turn, starting with the dealer's left-hand neighbour. On your turn, you may either keep your card (turn it face up if it's a King) or demand to swap it with that of your left-hand neighbour. The latter may only refuse if they hold a King, in which case they show it and say 'Cuckoo!'</li>

<li>Showdown: When it comes round to the dealer, he or she may either keep their card or cut a replacement from the pack. The cards are then revealed, and whoever has the lowest loses a life. Players tying for lowest all lose a life.</li>

<li>Optional rule: If the dealer rejects their card, and then cuts a King, it counts lowest of all, and only the dealer loses a life.</li>

<li>Game: The overall loser is the first to lose three lives.</li>
</ul>

ROLLING STONE

A simple game that threatens to go on for ever.

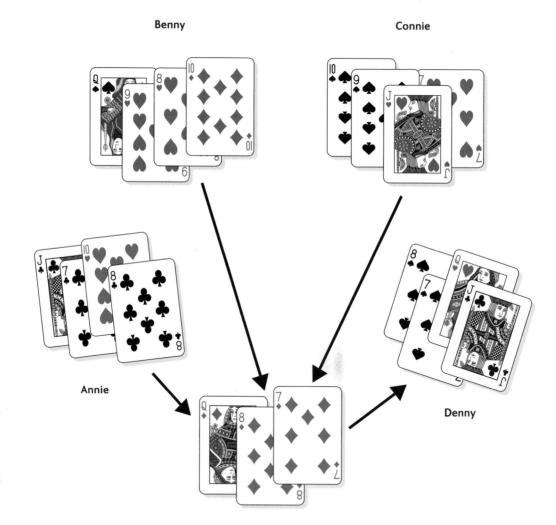

Above: *Denny has no Diamond to add to the trick, so he must pick up all three cards, add them to his hand, and lead to the next.*

- **Players**: Three to six.

- **Cards**: 52, running from high to low A K Q J 10 9 8 7 6 5 4 3 2. Ideally, the number used should be eight times the number of players, so strip out as many lower numerals as necessary to produce this effect.

- **Deal**: Deal eight cards to each player.

- **Object**: To be the first to run out of cards.

- **Play**: The dealer's left-hand neighbour leads to the first trick. The others must follow suit if possible. If you can't follow suit, you must take all the cards so far played, add them to your hand and lead to a new trick. Otherwise the trick ends when everyone has contributed a card. Whoever played the highest card wins the trick, throws it away, and leads to the next.

- **Winning**: Play ends when somebody wins by playing the last card from their hand.

SIFT SMOKE

The opposite of Rolling Stone: in Sift Smoke (also called Linger Longer) the aim is to avoid running out of cards.

❖ **Players:** Three to six.

❖ **Cards:** 52, running from high to low A K Q J 10 9 8 7 6 5 4 3 2.

❖ **Deal:** Deal 10 each if three play, 7 if four, 6 if five, or 5 if six. Show the dealer's last card to fix the trump suit, and stack the rest face down as a stock.

❖ **Object:** To be the last player left with any cards in hand.

❖ **Play:** The dealer's left-hand neighbour leads to the first trick, and the winner of each trick leads to the next. You must follow suit if you can, but may otherwise play any card. The trick is taken by the highest card of the suit led, or by the highest trump if any are played.

❖ **Drawing:** Tricks are worthless and thrown away, but the winner of each trick (only) draws the top card from the stock and adds it to their hand before leading to the next. As players run out of cards, they drop out of play, and the winner is the last player left with any cards in hand. If all play their last card to the same trick, the winner of the trick wins the game.

❖ **Renewing the stock:** If the stock runs out before anyone wins, gather up all the tricks, shuffle them, and lay their cards face down as a new stock.

❖ **Winning:** The winner scores a point for each card they have left.

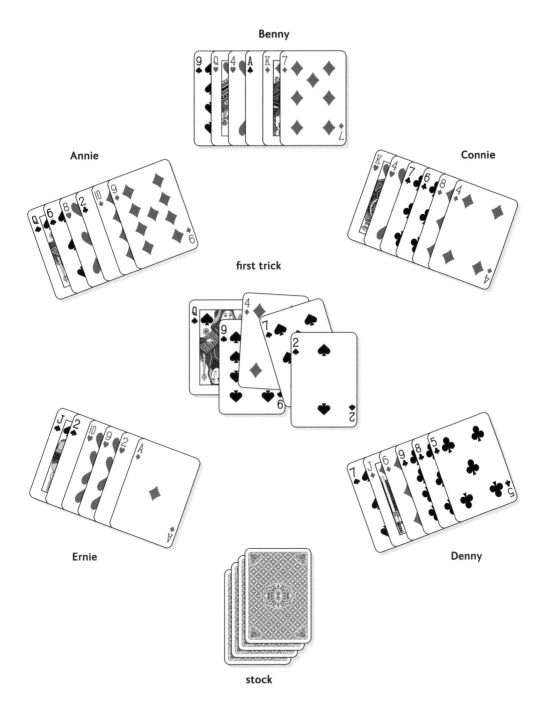

Above: *Ernie dealt and turned up J♠ for trumps. Annie leads with a high trump (not a particularly good idea), and all but Connie follow suit. Annie now draws a sixth card, leaving the others with only five each.*

CHEAT

Or, more accurately, Liar. Also called I Doubt It.

❖ **Players:** Three to seven.

❖ **Cards:** 52.

❖ **Deal:** Deal all the cards out. It doesn't matter if some have more than others.

❖ **Object:** To be the first to shed all your cards.

Annie	Benny	Connie	Denny
Aces!	Twos!	Threes!	Fours!

...and this is what they actually did put out:

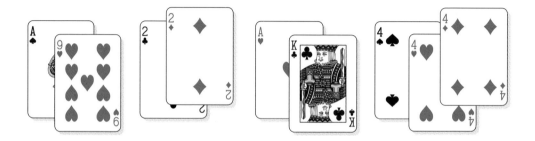

Above: *Annie doesn't believe that Denny really put out three Fours and calls 'Cheat!'. Denny proves her wrong, so Annie must add all nine cards to her hand and it's now Denny's turn to play.*

Play: The dealer's left-hand neighbour takes one, two, three or four cards from the hand and lays them face down on the table, saying 'Aces'. The second does likewise, saying 'Twos', and so on up to 'Kings'. Unless challenged, the cards so played are left in a pile on the table.

Challenge: Anyone may challenge an announcement by saying 'Cheat!', or 'I doubt it.' The cards just played are then turned up. If they are not all they were said to be, whoever played them must take all the cards in the pile and add them to their hand; otherwise, they must be taken by the challenger. Whoever wins a challenge is the next to play.

Winning: The winner is the first player to run out of cards.

BELIEVE IT OR NOT

This cross between Cheat and Old Maid is a Russian game called Verish' ne Verish', meaning 'Trust me or don't'.

❖ **Players:** Two to six.

❖ **Cards:** 52, but if only two or three play, reduce the pack to 36 cards by stripping out all numerals from 2 to 5.

❖ **Deal:** Remove a random card from the pack without looking at it and lay it face down to one side. Deal the rest round as far as they will go.

❖ **Play:** The dealer's left-hand neighbour places from one to four cards face down on the table and declares them to be of any rank – for example 'Jacks'. Each in turn thereafter must either:

- Play one or more cards face down and declare the same rank as the previous player, or

- Say 'Don't believe you!' and turn that player's cards face up.

The challenger, if mistaken, or the challenged player, if caught lying, must take up all the cards so far played and add them to their hand. They may then remove any set of four matching cards from their hand, show them, and discard them face down. This player's left-hand neighbour then starts the next round.

Ending: When all complete sets of four are eliminated, the player left with three of the initially discarded rank is the loser.

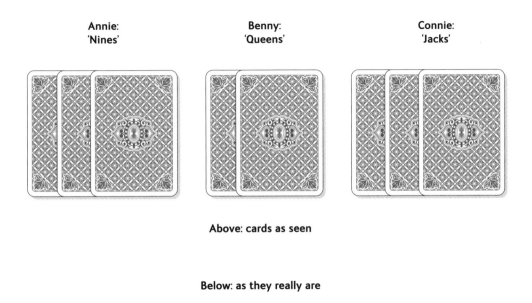

Annie: Benny: Connie:
'Nines'   'Queens'   'Jacks'

Above: cards as seen

Below: as they really are

Above: Annie and Benny play respectively three and two cards and are not challenged, thereby successfully getting rid of an extra card. Connie's claim of 'three Jacks' is challenged by Annie, who now has to add them to her hand for an unsuccessful challenge.

GO FISH!

A slighter game than Go Boom.

❖ **Players**: Three to seven.

❖ **Cards**: 52.

❖ **Deal**: Deal five cards each, stack the rest face down.

❖ **Object**: To be the first to run out of cards by laying them down in sets of four of a kind (four Aces, Tens, Jacks and so on).

Above: Annie now has to add a card from the stock to her hand and it's Benny's turn to ask.

Play: Starting with the dealer's left-hand neighbour, you each in turn ask any one other player for a particular card by name. It must be one of which you hold at least one match. For example, if you ask for Q♦, you must already hold at least one Queen.

If the player addressed has that card, they must surrender it to you in exchange for one of yours that you don't want. You then get another turn and may ask someone else (or the same player) for another card.

Go fish! When somebody asks you for a card that you haven't got, you say 'Go fish!' This forces the questioner to draw a card from the stock and add it to their hand. It then becomes your turn to ask someone for a card.

Four alike: Whenever you get four of a kind, you lay them face down on the table.

Ending: Keep going till one player runs out of cards. If the stock runs out first, anyone told to 'Go fish!' just ends their turn without drawing.

AUTHORS

Simpler than Go Fish!, ancestral to Happy Families and the basis for modern games with 'Quartet' in the title.

❖ **Players**: Two to four.

❖ **Cards**: 52.

❖ **Deal**: Deal all the cards out as far as they will go. It doesn't matter if some players get more than others.

✦ **Object**: To shed your cards by discarding them in 'books'. A book is four of a kind (Aces, Kings and so on).

✦ **Play:** Starting with the dealer's left-hand neighbour, you each in turn ask any one other player for cards of a particular rank, for example 'Jacks'. It must be one of which you hold at least one other of the same rank.

If the player addressed has any of that rank they must hand them over to you. You then get another turn and may ask someone else (or the same player) for another rank. If they don't hold it, they say 'None' and it becomes their turn to play.

✦ **Ending:** Whenever you make a 'book' — that is, all four of a given rank — you show them to the others and lay them down like a won trick. The winner is the first to run out of cards, whether by giving them away or discarding them in fours.

Annie

Benny

Connie

Denny

Above: If Annie asks Denny to give her Nines, she would immediately complete a 'book' of four and play again. She is more likely to ask for Aces or Sixes, but if it's Connie she asks, she won't get anything.

RACING DEMON

A traditional favourite, nowadays played under the name Pounce, or (in America) Nerts. Basically, everyone plays their own game of Demon (*see* page 160), but they can interact with each other. It has many variations and alternative rules.

✤ **Players**: Three to four, but the more players there are, the bigger the table you'll need.

✤ **Cards**: One 52-card pack per player. Each one must be distinguishable from the others by back design or colour, otherwise it will take hours to shuffle them back into complete packs! Everybody starts by shuffling their own pack and arranging it as follows:

✥ **Deal:** Deal 13 cards face down in a pile. This pile is your Demon pile, or Pounce pile, or Nerts pile, or whatever else you call the game. I will call it your off pile, because your aim is to be the first to play off all its cards.

✥ **Your workspace:** Next, deal four cards face up in a row in front of you in your own 'workspace'. These are your 'upcards'.

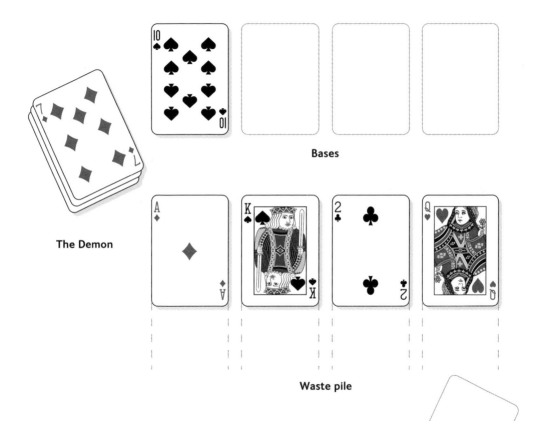

Bases

The Demon

Waste pile

Above: In this example, you must set the other Tens out as bases, as and when they appear, and build them all up in suit (via -Q-K-A-2-) to the Nines. Unusable cards go to the waste pile. The top card of the Demon and the waste pile are always available for building. Columns are to be built downwards in opposite colours. In this very improbable case, for example, you can start by playing A♦ to 2♣, then K♠ to A♦, then Q♥ to K♠, leaving three spaces, which you can fill with the top three cards of the Demon.

- ❖ **Common area:** The middle of the table between your individual workspaces is a common playing area. It should be large enough to contain more than four piles of cards.

- ❖ **Play:** Your four upcards mark the start of four work piles, each of which will take additional cards spread face up towards you so all are visible. If any of these four is an Ace, play it to the common area and replace it with the top card of your pack, which you hold face downwards in one hand. If the top card of your off pile is an Ace, do likewise, and turn up the card beneath it.

- ❖ **Ace piles:** Each Ace set out in the common playing area acts as the foundation of a pile, which is to be built upwards in suit and sequence until it contains 13 cards, headed by a King. Anyone can play a card to one of these piles whenever they have the next highest card in sequence. If two try playing to the same pile at once, only the card that gets there first stays put; the other must be taken back.

- ❖ **Play:** When ready, you all start playing at once. The top card of your off pile, and the exposed card in each of your work piles, may be played to one of the Ace piles when it fits.

Building on work piles: The cards in your work piles are to be built downwards in alternating colours (for example, red Jack on black Queen). You can also transfer any card from one work pile to another, together with all the cards lying in alternating sequence on top of it, provided that the join follows the rule. For example, if the exposed card of one pile is **9♣**, and another pile contains **8♣**, with **7♣** and **6♣** on top, you can play these three to the black Nine.

If you empty a work pile, you can fill the space it leaves with any available card, whether from the off pile, another work pile, your hand, or your waste pile (when it gets going).

Your waste pile: When stuck, deal the top three cards of your pack face up to a single waste pile and consider the topmost card. If possible, you may play this to one of the Ace piles (upwards in suit) or to one of your work piles (downwards in alternating colours), thus revealing the next card for similar play. When stuck, deal the next three cards from your pack face up to the waste pile, and again make whatever plays you can.

When your pack contains only one or two cards, turn them over in the usual way; then, when you get stuck again, turn the waste pile upside down and take it in hand to form a new pack to play from.

Getting stuck: If everyone gets stuck, whether unable or unwilling to make a move, everyone turns their waste pile to form a new pack, then transfers the top card of their pack to the bottom before continuing play.

Completed Ace piles: When an Ace pile is complete, with a King on top, turn it face down. Nothing else can be played to it.

Going out: Play ceases when somebody plays the last card from their off pile and calls 'Out!' (or 'Nerts', or whatever). Everybody then scores 1 point for each card they managed to work into the Ace piles (this is why it is necessary for everyone to have a distinctive pack), and deducts two points for each card left in their off pile.

Game: Play up to 100 points, or any other agreed target.

RICH MAN, POOR MAN

This Japanese game (Dai Fugō), ancestral to the Western game called President (and other, ruder things), is the simplest version of a whole family of related games.

✤ **Players**: Three to six.

✤ **Cards**: 53, including a Joker.

✤ **Card order:** The Joker is the highest card, followed by all the Twos, then Aces, Kings, and so on, down to Threes.

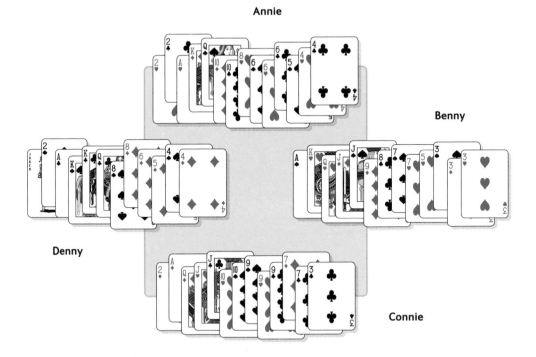

Above: *In this game players prefer to group their cards by face value rather than by rank. Annie could start with a single card, or with a pair of Fours, Sixes, Tens or Twos, or with three Sixes, or with a sequence of 4-5-6 or Q-K-A-2.*

- **Deal:** Anyone deals the first hand. Thereafter the loser of each hand deals to the next. Deal all the cards round as far as they will go.

- **Object:** By shedding all your cards, to become as rich as possible as often as possible.

- **Play:** Tricks may contain any number of cards. The dealer's left-hand neighbour leads to the first one. The lead may consist of any one of the following:

  - Any single card

  - A matched pair, such as 3–3 (the lowest) or 2–2 (highest)

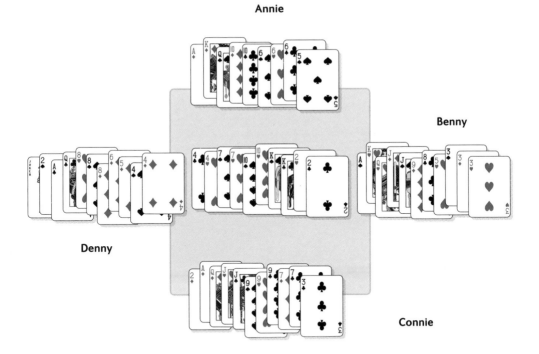

Above: *Annie leads with her pair of Fours, which Benny beats with Sevens, Connie with Tens, and Denny with Kings. Annie beats them all with her pair of Twos, which can't be beaten by Denny's 2-Joker as it is equal in rank, not higher. Annie might now continue by leading 6-6-6, and Connie would win this round with her Nines. Or she could lead her A-K-Q, which she would win, as no one has a higher sequence of three.*

- Three matched cards (a triplet)

- Four matched cards

- A sequence: that's three or more consecutive cards of the same suit, like **3,4,5♠** (the lowest) or **K,A,2♦** (highest).

Joker: The joker counts as any desired card in a pair, triplet, quartet or sequence. It doesn't beat the same combination composed of natural cards. For example, you can't beat **6,7,8♥** with **6,7♣**, **Joker** as they are equal in rank.

Following to a trick: On your turn to play to a trick already started, you may freely play or pass. Passing doesn't prevent you from playing to the same trick if the turn comes round to you again. If you don't pass, you must play the same number of cards and type of combination as the one led, and it must be higher than any other combination already played to the trick.

Keep going round till someone plays a card or combination that no one else can or will beat. Whoever then played last removes the trick from the table and starts a new one with a single card or combination of two or more.

✤ **Ending a round:** When one player runs out of cards, the others keep playing till only one is left in. Whoever ran out of cards first is the Very Rich Man, second the Rich Man, last the Poor Man, and the one left with cards in the hand is Very Poor Man. If only three play there, is no Poor Man.

✤ **Next deal:** The next deal is made by the Very Poor Man. Before play begins, this player gives the Very Rich Man the two highest cards he or she holds in exchange for the two lowest cards held by the Very Rich Man. The Very Poor Man then leads to the first trick.

✤ **Scoring:** The Japanese don't usually play for anything except the fun of being as rich as possible as often as possible, but it would make sense to score 2 points every time you finish up Very Rich, or 1 point whenever you are merely Rich.

✤ **Game:** Agree in advance how many deals to play, or a target score to play up to.

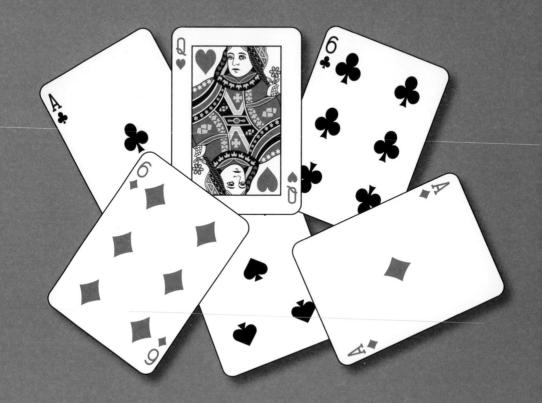

Your aim in these games is to collect, by various means, cards that match one another by rank or suit or both. Most of them belong to the Rummy family, whose general pattern is described overleaf. The others follow methods of their own that may or may not be based on Rummy. We'll describe these as we come to them.

MATCHING GAMES

RUMMY

Rummy is a general term for a large family of games in which you aim to collect matched sets of cards called melds.

There are two sorts of melds:

❖ **Sequence:** Three or more cards of the same suit and in numerical order. Ace can usually be high or low.

❖ **Set:** Three or more cards of the same rank.

This is the method of play common to most rummy games:

1. The dealer, after dealing each player seven cards, places the undealt cards face down in a pile called the stock, then turns its top card face up and places it beside the stock to form the discard or waste pile.

2. You each in turn draw either the top (face-down) card of the stock or the top (face-up) card of the waste pile and add it to your hand.

3. You discard any unwanted card face up to the waste pile.

4. You meld a set or sequence by laying it face up on the table. In some games you do this as you go along, in others you do it at the end.

5. In most games, you can add a card to an existing meld if it continues the sequence in either direction or belongs to the set. This is called 'laying off'. You can always lay off to a meld of your own, and in some games, can do so to other players' melds.

6. The first player to shed all their cards is said to 'go out', and this ends the game.

7. Cards left unmelded in other players' hands count against them. These are called 'deadwood'.

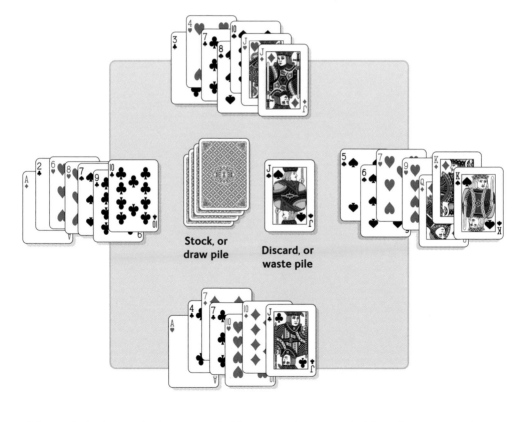

Above: *Each player is dealt seven cards. The remainder are stacked face down as a stock or draw pile, and its top card is turned up to start the discard or waste pile.*

BASIC RUMMY

This is the most widely played form of Rummy.

❖ **Players:** From two to seven, best with three to five.

❖ **Cards:** 52, but for more than four players, use two packs shuffled together. Jokers may be added. Thorough shuffling is essential.

❖ **Card order:** The order of the cards in sequences is Ace (low) 2 3 4 5 6 7 8 9 10 J Q K.

❖ **Deal:** Seven to each player (some prefer 10). Stack the rest face down as a draw pile, turn up its top card and place it next to the draw pile to start a discard pile.

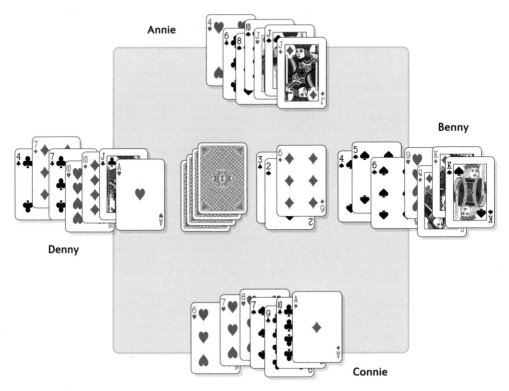

Above: *After one round of play.*

Below: Connie drew **5♥**, *discarded* **7♠**, *and 'went rummy' with sequences in Clubs and Hearts. Denny would dearly have loved to draw the* **7♠** *to make a set of Sevens, but cannot even lay off his* **J♣** *to Connie's sequence as he has not yet made a meld himself. Annie has three Jacks and Benny has a four-card sequence in Spades. Connie scores 26 for Annie's deadwood, 30 for Benny's and 53 for Denny's: total 109.*

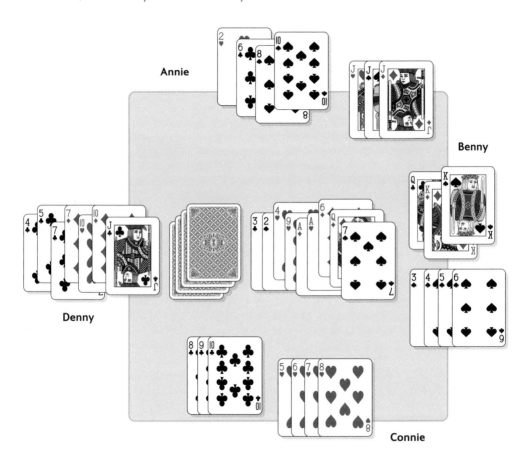

- **Object:** To run out of cards by playing them out in melds.

- **Play:** The dealer's left-hand neighbour starts. At each turn you draw the top card of either the draw or the discard pile, add it to your hand, and throw an unwanted card, face up, to the discard pile.

- **Melding**: After drawing and before discarding you may lay out in front of you three or more cards that form a set or sequence.

✤ **Laying off:** You may add a card to an existing meld belonging to you or another player if it continues the sequence in either direction, or belongs to the same set. But you may not lay off until you have already started a meld yourself.

✤ **Jokers:** Jokers, if included, are wild; they can be used to count as any card in a meld. A meld may not contain more than one Joker.

✤ **Renewing the draw pile:** If the last card gets taken from the draw pile, turn the discard pile face down to start a new one, and place its top card face up to start a new discard pile.

✤ **Going out:** You go out by playing your last remaining card, whether by using it in a meld or discarding it. This ends the game.

✤ **Scoring:** The player who went out scores the face value of all the cards remaining in other players' hands, counting Ace as 1, numerals at face value, face cards at 10 each, Jokers at 15 each.

✤ **Game:** The turn to deal passes to the left. Either play as many deals as there are players, or play up to an agreed target score, such as 50 or 100.

GIN RUMMY

This closely resembles its ancestor Rummy, and reached its heyday in the 1930s on Broadway and in Hollywood. Deceptively simple, it rewards thoughtful play.

❖ **Players**: Two.

❖ **Cards**: 52, Ace counts low (A, 2, 3) or high (Q, K, A).

❖ **Deal**: Ten each, in ones. Stack the rest face down as a draw pile, turn up its top card and place it next to the draw pile to start a discard pile. The top card of the discard pile is the upcard.

❖ **Object**: To be the first to 'knock' by laying out all or most of your cards in melds. Unlike basic Rummy, you don't make melds piecemeal as you go along.

❖ **Play**: The non-dealer may take the upcard or pass. If they pass, the dealer has the same option. If the dealer also passes, the non-dealer starts by drawing the top card of the draw pile. Play then continues as in Basic Rummy. If you take the upcard, you may not discard it on the same turn.

❖ **Knocking:** You can end the game by knocking when:

- You can make one or more melds using all the cards in your hand after making a final discard (this is called 'going gin'), or

- When you can meld most of your cards and those remaining unmelded have a total face value of 10 or less, counting Ace as 1, others at face value and faces at 10 each.

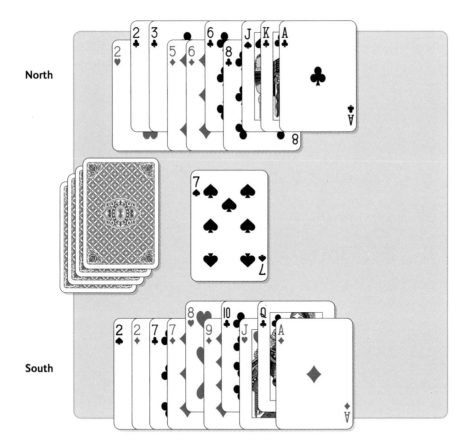

*Above: North doesn't want the **7♠**, but South does (to make three Sevens) and discards J♥. North takes the J♥ (to make a pair) and discards 2♥. South takes that and discards 8♥. Then, for the first time in this game, North draws the top card of the stock.*

❖ **Scoring**: For going gin, the knocker scores the face value of all the opponent's cards that can't be formed into melds, plus a bonus of 25. If the knocker did not go gin, the opponent may then make any melds possible, and lay off any unmelded cards that can be matched against the knocker's melds. The knocker then scores the difference between the values of both players' deadwood. If the knocker's deadwood equals or exceeds that of the opponent, the opponent scores that difference plus a bonus of 25 for 'undercut'.

• **Game**: The deal alternates and the winner is the first to reach 100 points. Both players then add 25 for each hand they won, and the winner adds a further 100 for the game.

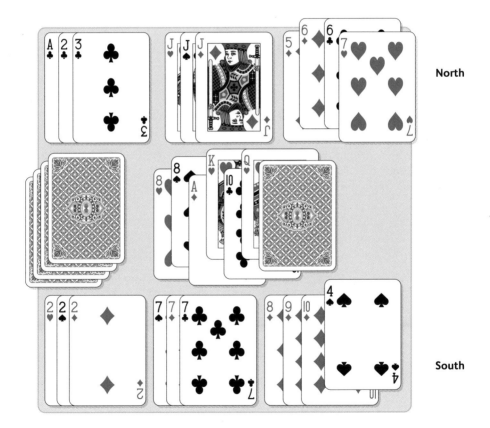

Above: *South knocks by making a final discard (Q♣) face down, and the two final hands are revealed. South has two sets of three and a sequence of three, and only 4 points against. North has one set and one sequence of three, and can lay off the 7♥ to South's Sevens. South scores 17 – 4 = 13, the difference between the deadwood in both hands.*

BRUMMY

Rummy in two dimensions! For two to four players.

- **Cards:** 52 (or, if more than four play, 104), ranking A K Q J 10 9 8 7 6 5 4 3 2 in each suit.

- **Deal:** Deal nine cards each, stack the rest face down as a stock, and turn its top card face up to start a discard pile.

- **Object:** To transform your hand of nine cards into one that will produce the highest-scoring grid of 3 x 3 cards, scores being made for Cribbage combinations in each of its eight lines (three rows, three columns and two diagonals). From highest to lowest, the combinations and their scores are:

  - Prial (pair royal): three cards of the same rank, e.g. A-A-A. Scores 6

  - Running flush: three cards in suit and sequence, e.g. A-2-3 of Hearts. Scores 6

  - Flush: three cards of the same suit, not all in sequence. Scores 3

  - Run: three cards in sequence, not all of one suit. Scores 3

  If using 104 cards, two identical cards must not appear in the same row, column or diagonal, otherwise that line scores 0.

- **Play:** Play by drawing and discarding, as in Basic Rummy.

- **Knocking:** When you think you have the best hand, make your last discard face down. Everyone else then gets one more turn.

- **Ending and scoring:** You each arrange your nine cards into a grid of 3 x 3, seeking to score as high as possible. This example (right) scores a total of 20. Whoever makes the highest score adds a bonus of 10. Play up to any agreed target.

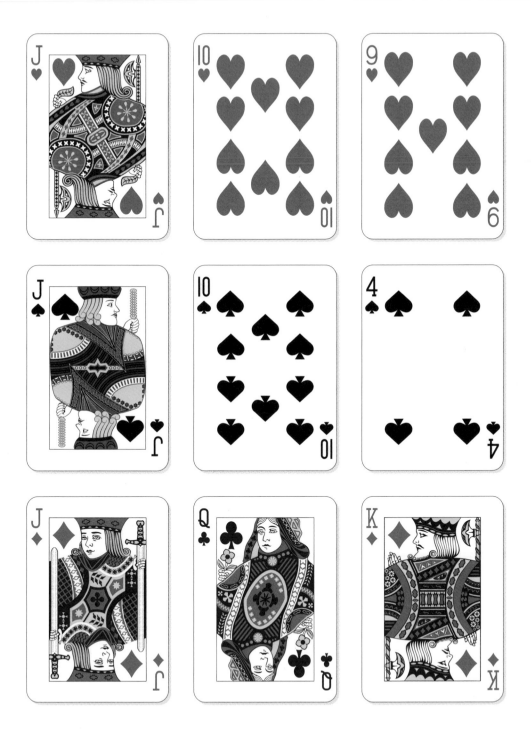

Above: *This hand scores for the horizontal rows 6 + 3 + 3 and for the vertical columns 6 + 2 + 0, making a total of 20 points.*

VATICAN

This is the version on which the popular game of Rummikub is based.

❖ **Players:** Two to five, best with three to four.

❖ **Cards:** 106, consisting of two 52-card packs and two Jokers.

❖ **Deal:** 13 cards each, in ones. Stack the rest face down to form a draw pile. There is no discard pile.

❖ **Object:** To play all your cards from hand to melds on the table.

❖ **Melds:** Sequence order is A 2 3 4 5 6 7 8 9 10 J Q K A. Ace counts both high and low, so K, A, 2 is allowed. Sets of three or four must not contain two of the same suit.

❖ **Play:** At each turn, you either draw the top card or play at least one card from your hand to melds on the table. If you can't play when the draw pile is empty, you must pass.

Your first meld must be a sequence. After that, you may add one or more cards to the table on this and any subsequent turn, and arrange or rearrange melds as you please, so long as you end your turn leaving all cards on the table arranged in melds of at least three cards each.

- **Jokers:** Jokers are wild. A Joker on the table may be replaced by the card it represents, but may not then be taken up; it must be used somewhere as part of a meld.

- **Ending:** If the draw pile empties before anyone goes out, you must keep playing as long as possible or pass if you can't. The winner is the first to play their last card.

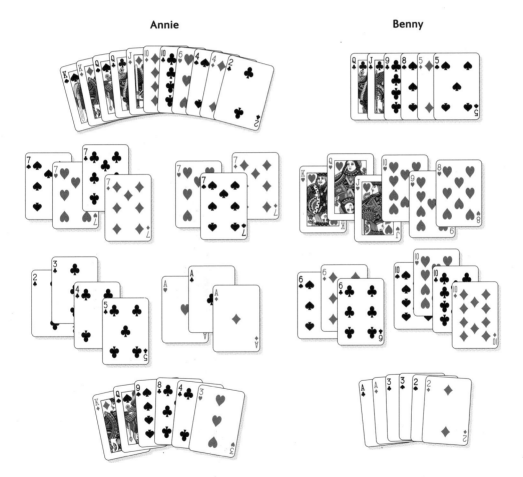

Above: A game in progress. Annie could lay off Kings and Queens to the King and Queen taken from the Heart sequence, and 6♥ to the Sixes. Benny could make a sequence of five Clubs by robbing **10♣** from the set of four.

THREE THIRTEEN

A modern American game.

- **Players:** Two to four.

- **Cards:** 52 if two play, otherwise 104 (two packs). Ace counts low.

- **Deal:** Three each in the first round, four in the second, then five, six and so on up to 13 in the eleventh and last. Stack the rest face down as a draw pile and place its top card face up to start a discard pile.

- **Object:** To form all your cards into melds of sequences or sets.

- **Wild cards:** A wild card can be used to represent any desired card. In the first round, Threes are wild, in the second Fours, and so on up to Kings in the eleventh round.

- **Play:** At each turn you take a card from the top of the draw or discard pile and discard one to the discard pile. You don't make melds until you can go out.

- **Going out:** You go out by making melds using all 10 cards and making a final discard. Everyone else then has one more turn and may also go out if they can.

❖ **Scoring**: If you haven't gone out, you score penalty points equal to the total face value of all the cards remaining in hand after making as many melds as you can.

❖ **Game**: The winner is the player with fewest penalty points at the end of the eleventh round.

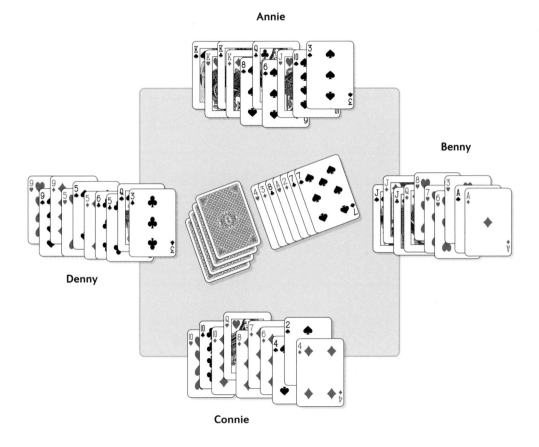

Annie

Benny

Denny

Connie

Above: *At the end of the tenth round, with Queens wild, Denny goes out by discarding* **7♠**. *Annie has four Kings and a sequence of three, including a wild Queen, and counts 23 points in penalties. Benny has three Jacks and Aces, one of them a wild Queen, and 3 points against (for the 3♥). Connie has three Tens and a sequence of four and counts 10 in penalties. However, each player gets one more turn, so Annie takes the* **7♠** *for her Spade sequence and extends it by shifting the wild* **Q♣**. *If she discards her* **J♥**, *to reduce her penalties to 13, Benny will take it to add to his Jacks and discard an Ace to reduce his penalties by 1 point. Finally, Connie can take the discarded Ace and swap it for a Four, thus reducing her penalties to 7.*

FIFTY-ONE

A family game from Japan, where it's called Goju Ichi.

❖ **Players**: Two to five, best with four.

❖ **Cards**: 52.

❖ **Values**: Aces count as 11 each, face cards 10, numerals 2 to 10 at face value.

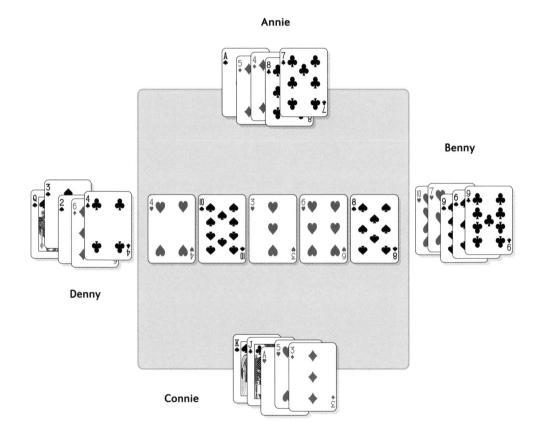

Above: *Annie (top) takes* **10♠** *and discards* **8♣**, *Benny takes* **8♠** *in exchange for* **9♣**, *Connie takes* **6♥** *for* **3♦**. *Denny doesn't like the cards on offer so sweeps the five table cards away and deals 5 more.*

Deal: Deal five cards to each player and five face up to the table, then stack the rest face down as a draw pile.

Object: To finish with the best possible score, made by counting the total value of all the cards of one suit and subtracting the values of all other cards.

Play: At each turn you take one of the table cards and replace it with a different card from your hand. Before doing so, you may (except on your first turn) clear the table cards away and replace them with five new cards from the draw pile. When the draw pile is empty, the discards are shuffled and formed into a new one.

Stopping: After picking up and discarding, you may call 'Stop!' if you think you have the best hand – the one with the highest value of cards in any one suit. Everyone else then gets one more turn.

Scoring: The value of your hand is the total value of all the cards of one suit minus the total values of all other cards. This may result in a negative score. The winner is the player with the highest score, or an opponent who has an equal or higher score than the stopper.

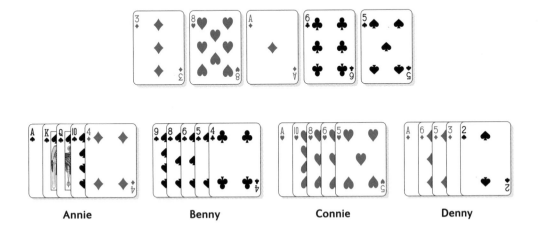

Above: *The new table cards are shown above. Denny takes A♦ in exchange for Q♠. After one or two more rounds, Annie stops the game, counting 41 for her top Spades minus 4♦, making 37. Benny counts 28 – 4 = 24 and Denny 25 – 2 = 23. But Connie beats them all with her solid Hearts counting 40.*

ABSTRAC

A very simple game, but one that rewards careful thought.

❖ **Players:** Two.

❖ **Cards:** 24, consisting of A K Q J 10 9 in each suit.

❖ **Deal:** Shuffle the cards thoroughly and deal them all out in a row, face up and slightly overlapping, as shown.

❖ **Object:** To take cards that form matching sets and sequences, as in Rummy, but without taking more cards than absolutely necessary.

❖ **Play:** The non-dealer examines the layout and decides whether to play first or second. If second, the dealer must play first.

You each in turn draw either one, two or three consecutive cards from the uncovered end of the row (from **A♠** in this example) until none remain. Place the ones you take face up on the table before you, clearly arranged by suit and rank, so your opponent can always see what you have taken so far.

❖ **Score:** The scoring combinations are sets of three or more cards of the same rank and sequences of three or more cards of the same suit. A card belonging to both types can be scored twice, once in a set and once in a sequence. Your score for the deal consists of these two part-scores multiplied together:

First, for combinations, score as follows:

- sets: three of a kind 2 points, four of a kind 8 points

- suit sequences: of three = 3, four = 4, five = 6, six = 12 points.

Next, total your score for combinations and multiply this by the total number of cards taken by your opponent. This gives you your score for the deal.

❖ **Game:** Play up to any agreed target, such as 1,000 points.

Above: *An initial layout. Cards are taken one, two or three at a time from right to left.*

Non-dealer   **Dealer**

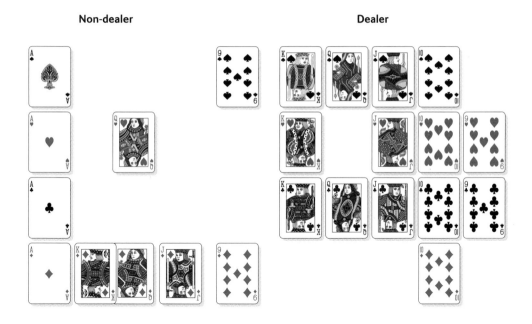

Above: *Non-dealer played first and took 10 cards, scoring 8 for the Aces and 4 for the Diamond sequence, total 12, times the 14 that Dealer took, making 168. Dealer scored 8 for the Tens, 2 each for the trios of Kings and Jacks, plus 4 for the Spades sequence, 3 for the Hearts and 6 for the Clubs, for a total of 25, times Non-dealer's 10 cards = 250. The results would have been different if they had taken different numbers of cards at each turn. For example, if each player always took one card Dealer would win by 96 to 60; if two, Non-dealer would win by 144 to 120; and if three, Non-dealer would win by 96 to 84.*

CRIBBAGE

Cribbage, or Crib, can lay claim to being the English national card game and is popular throughout the English-speaking world. It was developed from an older game by Sir John Suckling, a courtier (and later enemy) of Charles I. Here is the modern version for two players. It's a counting and card-matching game combined.

❖ **Cards**: 52.

❖ **Values**: Ace counts as 1, numerals at face value, faces 10 each.

❖ **Other equipment**: A cribbage board, easily obtainable from large stationers or game shops, or you can write scores down as you go along.

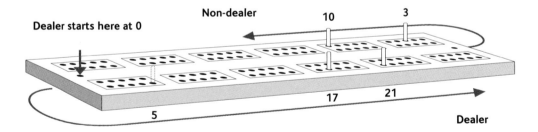

Above: *Using a Cribbage board: Scoring is recorded by using two pegs, the first initially in the start hole (0), the second off the board. In this example, Dealer scored first 5, then 12, then 4. So the first peg moved to 5, then the second 12 ahead of it to show 17, then the first again 4 ahead to show 21. Pegging continues up the outer and down the inner row of holes, then back round again. Eventually, it will be replaced in the start hole to show the final score of 121 – unless, of course, Non-dealer gets there first.*

❖ **Deal:** Whoever cuts the lower card (Ace lowest) deals first. The deal then alternates. Deal six cards each in ones.

❖ **Object:** To score 121 over several deals. Points are scored for making card combinations and playing cards to a count of up to 31.

❖ **Discarding:** You each make two discards face down to form a four-card 'crib', which will eventually count for the dealer. In discarding, you both aim to keep a hand of four cards that form scoring combinations. The dealer will throw combinable cards and the non-dealer non-combinable cards to the crib. The crib cards are placed together face down and must not be looked at yet.

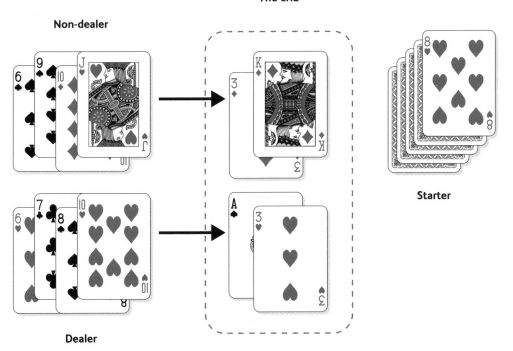

Above: In discarding to the crib, Non-dealer has kept fifteen (6 + 9) and his three-card run (9-10-J) and put two hopefully unhelpful cards into Dealer's crib. Dealer has kept her fifteen (7 + 8) and run of three (6-7-8) and put in the crib two cards that might form part of a low run.

✤ **Combinations:** The combinations and their scores are:

- Fifteen (2): two or more cards totalling 15 in face value, counting Ace as 1, numerals as marked, face cards 10 each

- Pair (2): two cards of the same rank

- Prial (pair royal) (6): three of the same rank

- Double pair royal (12): four of the same rank

- Run (one per card): three or more cards in ranking order

- Flush: four cards of the same suit in one hand.

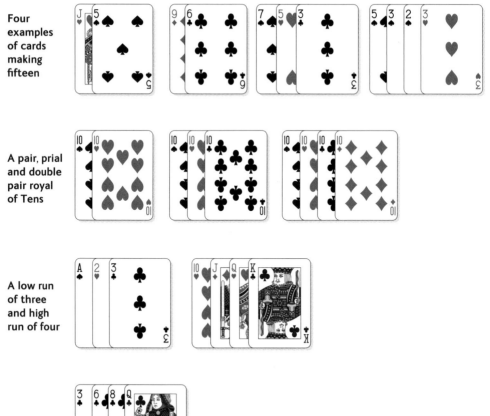

Four examples of cards making fifteen

A pair, prial and double pair royal of Tens

A low run of three and high run of four

A flush in Clubs

Above: Examples of scoring combinations.

Below: In this deal, there are three rounds of counting. In the first, Dealer pegs 2 for making 15, Non-dealer 2 for pairing the Six, and Dealer 2 for making 31. In the second, Dealer cannot play to 28 without going over 31. The third just consists of Dealer's last remaining card. The players then count their hands. Non-dealer counts 'Fifteen 2 (for 9 + 6), run of three (9-10-J), plus 1 for his nob (J♥) = 16'. Dealer counts 'Fifteen 2 (for 7 + 8), run of three 5 (for 7-8-9)'. Dealer then turns the crib (see page 111) and counts 'Fifteen 2 (for A + 3 + 3 + 8), pair 4 (3 + 3) – a rather disappointing result.

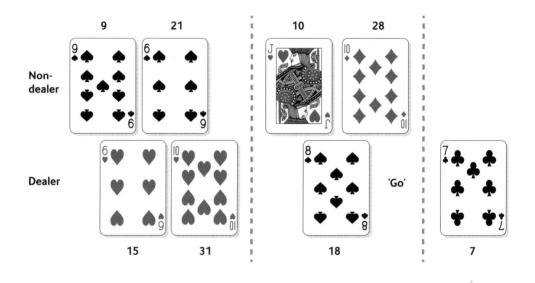

✤ **Starter:** The non-dealer lifts the top half of the undealt pack. The dealer removes the top card of the bottom half and puts it face up on top as the starter. If it's a Jack, the dealer pegs 2 'for his heels', provided no card has yet been played.

✤ **Play**: Starting with the non-dealer, you each in turn play a card face up to the table in front of you and announce the total face value of all cards so far played by both.

✤ **Scoring for totals:** For making the count exactly 15, you peg 1 point. You must add a card if able to do so without exceeding 31. If you can't, you say 'Go'. The other then adds as many more cards as possible without exceeding 31 and scores 1 for the go, or 2 for making 31 exactly. If either of you has any cards left, you turn face down all the cards played so far, and the next in turn to play starts a new count. When one player runs out of cards, the other continues alone.

❖ **Scoring for pairs and runs:** Points are also pegged for pairs and runs made by cards laid out successively in the play. A card matching the rank of the previous one played scores 2 for the pair; if the next played also matches, it scores 6; and the fourth, if it matches, 12.

If you play a card that completes an uninterrupted run of three or more in conjunction with the cards just played, the run is scored at the rate of 1 per card.

Here's an example: Annie plays 5, Benny 7, Annie 6 and pegs 3 for the run. If Benny then plays 4 or 8 he pegs 4. If he played 2 he would peg nothing, having broken the sequence; but Annie could then play 3 and re-form it for 6.

Runs need not be played in order. For example, if the first four cards played are A, 4, 2, 3, then whoever played last scores 4 for the run. Adding a Five would make it a run of five, while a Four would re-create a run of three. However, a run is broken by the interruption of a paired card. For example, in the consecutive play of 6, 7, 7, 8, the second Seven prevents the Eight from completing a run of three.

❖ **The show:** Each player, starting with the non-dealer, picks up their four hand cards and spreads them face up. Counting these and the starter as a five-card hand, you then score for any and all combinations it may contain – fifteens, pairs, prials, runs and flushes. A given card may be used in more than one combination. It may even be used more than once in the same combination, provided that at least one other associated card is different each time.

Here's an example: **6♠ 7♠ 7♥ 8♣ 9♦** scores 2 for each distinct card combination totalling 15 (**6♠ 9♦**, **7♥ 8♣**, **7♠ 8♦**) 2 for the pair of Sevens, and 4 for each run of four (**6♠ 7♠ 8♣ 9♦**, **6♠ 7♥ 8♣ 9♦**). Announce your scores like this: 'Fifteen 2, 4, 6; pair 8; fours 16'.

❖ **Scoring for flushes:** A flush (cards of the same suit) counts as 4, or 5 if its suit matches the starter's. A player holding the Jack of the same suit as the starter also pegs 1 'for his nob'. (If the starter is a Jack, neither player reckons for his nob, as it is overridden by the 2 'for his heels'.)

❖ **Counting the crib:** Finally, the dealer turns the crib face up and pegs for it as a five-card hand. The scoring is the same as for a hand, except that a flush only counts if all five are in suit.

❖ **Winning:** The winner is the first player to reach a total of 121 pegged points.

CRIBBAGE FOR FOUR

For many years Cribbage was the only card game legally playable in British pubs, and pubs remain the venues for various regional Cribbage leagues. The four-player version is widely preferred.

❖ **Players**: Four play in two partnerships of two each.

❖ **Deal**: Deal five cards each, and discard one each to the crib.

❖ **Play**: The dealer's left-hand neighbour leads to the first count and is the first to count the value of their hand. Pegging is done by the dealer's and leader's partners.

❖ **Scoring**: Each partnership scores the amount made by both its members.

These are the most widely played group of games in the West, if not throughout the world. Whist, in its many different forms, is the classic example. A 'trick' consists of one card played by each player in turn. Whoever plays the highest or best card wins them all. The person who 'leads' to a trick (plays the first card) can play any card they choose. The others must then 'follow' suit – that is, play one of the same suit – if they can, and if not, they can play a 'trump' card (beating any non-trump or 'plain-suit' card).

TRICK-TAKING GAMES

GENERAL RULES OF TRICK-TAKING GAMES

The following features and rules are typical but may vary in detail from game to game.

Players: Typically four, sitting crossways in two partnerships, but there are also versions for any number from two to seven. The players drawing the lowest two cards become partners against those drawing the highest.

Cards: 52, ranking from high to low A K Q J 10 9 8 7 6 5 4 3 2.

Deal: Whoever drew the highest card deals first, and the turn to deal passes to the left around the table.

Trumps: The trump suit is often that of the last card dealt, which is turned face up so everyone can see it. In more advanced games, players 'bid' for the right to choose a trump suit in return for undertaking to win the most tricks using that suit as trump.

Object: Usually to win the most tricks, but in some games to avoid winning any at all (technically called misère, misery or miz) or to avoid winning certain cards in tricks.

Play: The dealer's left-hand neighbour leads to the first trick and the winner of each trick leads to the next. Everyone else must follow suit if they can but may otherwise play any card. The trick is taken by the highest card of the suit led, or by the highest trump if any are played. In partnership games it is usual for all the tricks taken by one side to be placed in front of the player who took their first one.

Below: *Tricks: A trick is one card from each player. Annie leads 8♣. The others must follow suit if possible. Benny plays **Q♣**, which beats the Eight. Connie has no Clubs and discards 4♥. Denny plays the Two. Benny therefore wins the trick and places it face down before him.*

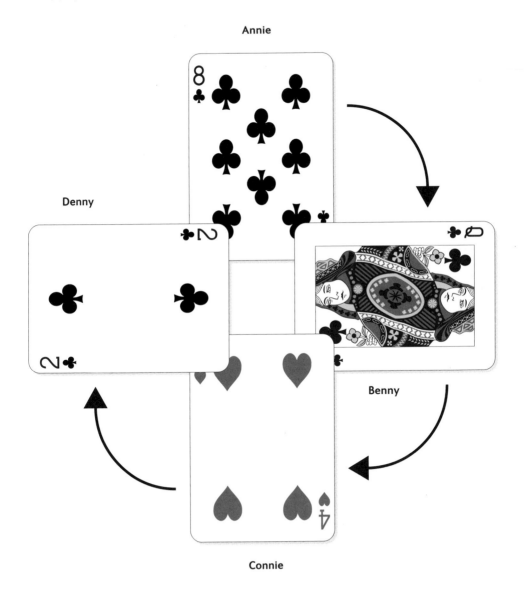

Annie

Denny

Benny

Connie

Above: *Trumps: One suit may be appointed as trump. A trump beats any non-trump card. If Hearts are trump, then Connie wins the trick with 4♥. If Denny had played, say, J♥, having no Clubs, then he would have won the trick by playing the highest trump.*

PARTNERSHIP WHIST

Whist is an old English card game that was popular throughout the Western world for 200 years, and often described as 'the king of card games'. It has given rise to many variants, and Contract Bridge is its most advanced descendant. Classical Partnership Whist, described here, is very simple but rewards skilful play.

❖ **Players:** Four, sitting crossways in two partnerships.

❖ **Cards:** 52, ranking from high to low A K Q J 10 9 8 7 6 5 4 3 2.

❖ **Deal:** 13 cards each, face down, in ones.

❖ **Trumps:** The last card is turned face up and its suit becomes the trump. When it has been seen, it is added to the dealer's hand.

❖ **Object:** To win the most tricks.

❖ **Play:** The dealer's left-hand neighbour leads to the first trick and the winner of each trick leads to the next. You must follow suit if you can, but may otherwise play any card. The trick is taken by the highest card of the suit led, or by the highest trump if any are played.

❖ **Score:** The side winning most tricks scores 1 point for each trick taken above seven.

- **Honours:** Scoring for honours is traditional, but may be ignored. If counted, at end of play a side which held most of the four highest trumps (whether or not in the same hand) adds 2 points if they held three, or 4 if they held four. Honours are not counted if the side that held them is 1 point short of winning the game.

- **Game:** The winning side counts a single game point if the other made 3 or 4 points, a double if the other made only 1 or 2, a treble if the other made no score. The first side to win two games adds 2 game points for the 'rubber'.

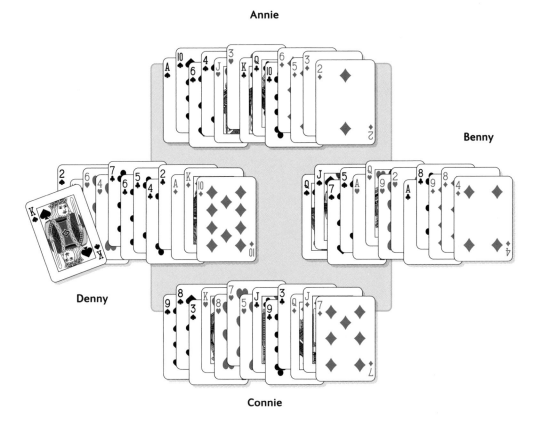

Above: Denny dealt and turned up K♠ as his last card, making Spades the trump suit. Annie will lead to the first trick. If honours are scored at the end of play, Denny and Benny will score one point for holding between them three of the top four trumps. In this deal Annie and Connie won four tricks to Benny and Denny's nine.

GERMAN WHIST

The two-player version is traditionally called German Whist.

✤ **Deal:** 13 cards each, in ones.

✤ **Trumps:** Stack the undealt cards face down as a draw pile but turn the top card face up to establish trumps.

Below: Zandy dealt 13 cards each and turned 3♣ to set the trump suit. Yvonne might lead K♥, win the trick, and draw the low trump. Or she might prefer to lead 3♥ and lose the trick in hope of drawing a better card from the draw pile.

✤ **Play:** The non-dealer leads to the first trick and the rules of trick play are as for Partnership Whist. The winner of each trick takes the top card of the draw pile into hand, waits for the other to draw the next, then turns up the next top card. (But this does not change the trump suit.) When the draw pile is empty, keep playing till you run out of cards.

✤ **Game:** The winner is the player who takes most of the 26 tricks. In some circles, it is whoever wins most of the last 13 tricks.

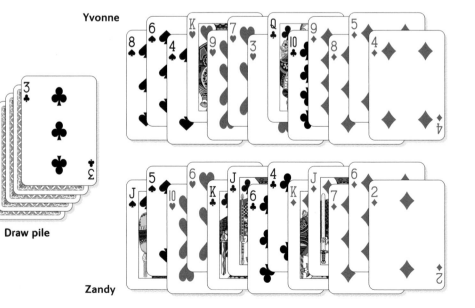

Yvonne

Draw pile

Zandy

DUTCH WHIST

Also called Bismarck, this is for three players.

✤ **Cards**: As for Partnership Whist.

✤ **Deal**: As the dealer you take the top four cards yourself, then deal 16 cards to each player one at a time (including yourself), then discard any four unwanted cards from your own hand. A game is 12 deals, with each player dealing in turn, and the dealer's left-hand neighbour leading to the first trick.

✤ **First deal**: Play with no trump. The dealer scores 8 less than the number of tricks he or she took, and each opponent 4 less.

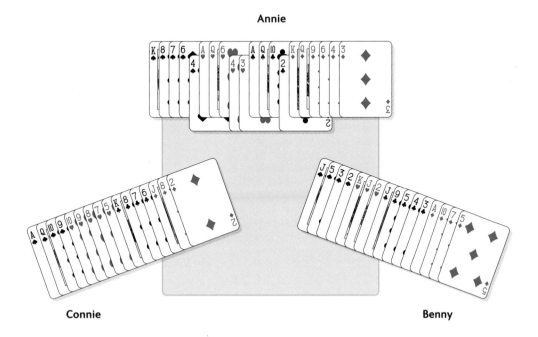

Above: *Dealer (Annie) discards four low cards before play (4♠, 4-3♥, 2♣) and Benny leads to the first trick. This being the first round, the deal is played without a trump suit. Benny and Connie each win five tricks, scoring 1 point, and Annie wins six, scoring minus 2 points (6-8).*

❖ **Second deal**: As before, but with a trump selected by cutting the pack before dealing.

❖ **Third deal:** As before, but with trumps announced by the dealer before their left-hand neighbour leads to the first trick.

❖ **Fourth deal:** Misère. No trump; aim to lose tricks. The dealer scores 4 less, and each opponent 6 less, than the number of tricks they won.

❖ **Game:** These deals are repeated in the same order. The overall winner is whoever won the most tricks.

KNOCKOUT WHIST

A very popular game for two to seven players, also called Trumps or Scrounge. Rules vary. These are the simplest.

Deal: Deal seven cards each, face down, in ones. Stack the rest face down.

Trumps: Turn the top card of the stack to fix the trump suit.

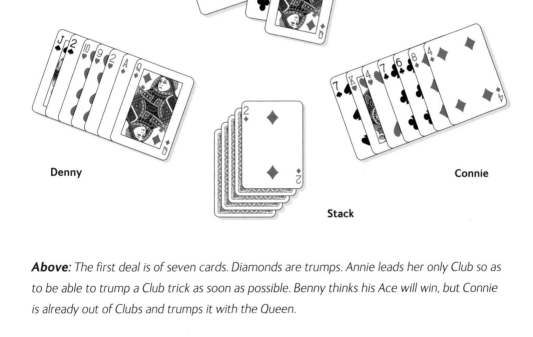

Above: The first deal is of seven cards. Diamonds are trumps. Annie leads her only Club so as to be able to trump a Club trick as soon as possible. Benny thinks his Ace will win, but Connie is already out of Clubs and trumps it with the Queen.

❖ **Object:** To win at least one trick in each deal, otherwise you are knocked out. The winner is the last person left in play.

❖ **Play:** In each round, the dealer leads to the first trick. Follow normal Whist rules. Anyone failing to take a trick is knocked out of the game.

❖ **Subsequent deals:** Whoever took the most tricks shuffles all 52 cards, deals six to each player, looks at their hand, announces trumps, and leads to the second round.

Play continues in this way, with those taking no tricks being knocked out, and the player taking most tricks dealing, choosing trumps and leading to the next. In case of a tie for most tricks, the tied player cutting the highest card deals next.

The number of cards dealt decreases by one on each deal, so that only one is dealt on the seventh round.

❖ **Game:** Whoever wins the last one-card trick wins the game.

❖ **Scoring:** Of many staking methods, the simplest has each active player putting a chip in the pot at the start of each deal, and the winner taking the pot.

OH HELL!

❖ **Players:** From three to six.   ❖ **Cards:** 52, as for Whist.

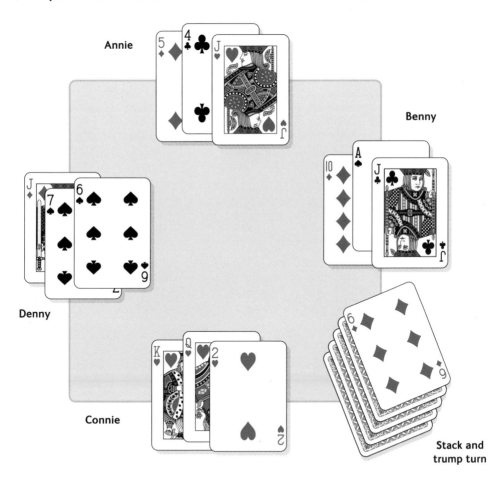

Above: In round 3 each receives three cards and Diamonds are trumps. Annie hopes to win a trick with her trump 5, Benny bids 2 with an Ace and a fairly high trump, and Connie bids 0. Denny would not be allowed to bid 0, but in any case expects his trump Jack to be good. In fact, Annie wins one and scores 11, Benny one and scores 1, Connie none and scores 10, Denny one and scores 1.

Deal: Deal one card to each player in the first round, two in the second, three in the third, and so on until there aren't enough to go round. Stack any undealt cards face down to one side.

Trumps: Turn the top card of the stack to fix trumps. If no card remains, play the round at no trump.

Announcements: Each in turn, starting at the dealer's left, announces ex-actly how many tricks he or she aims to win. The dealer, who bids last, may not bid a number that would enable everyone to fulfil their bid.

Play: Follow the rules of Whist.

Score: Score 1 point for each trick you won, plus a bonus of 10 if the number of tricks you won is exactly the number you bid.

SPADES

This very popular American game is played in many different ways. The following rules are typical rather than 'official'.

❖ **Players**: Four, sitting crossways in partnerships.

❖ **Cards**: 52, as for Whist.

❖ **Deal**: Deal 13 each, face down, one at a time.

❖ **Trumps**: Spades, always.

❖ **Bidding**: Each partnership undertakes to win a certain minimum number of tricks. First, the members of the non-dealer partnership discuss how many tricks they think they can win between them. They may each say how many they think they can, but may not give direct information about their cards. When their contract number is agreed, it is noted down, and the dealer's side does the same.

❖❖ **'Nil' bids:** If you think you can lose every trick individually you may declare 'nil'. Your partner then states how many they will go for. This establishes your side's contract, which is lost if the nil-bidder wins any tricks. Only one player per side may bid nil.

'Blind nil' is a nil bid made before a player looks at their cards. It is permitted only to a player whose side is losing by 100 or more points. In this case the nil-bidder passes two cards face down to their partner, who adds them to their hand and passes two cards face down in return.

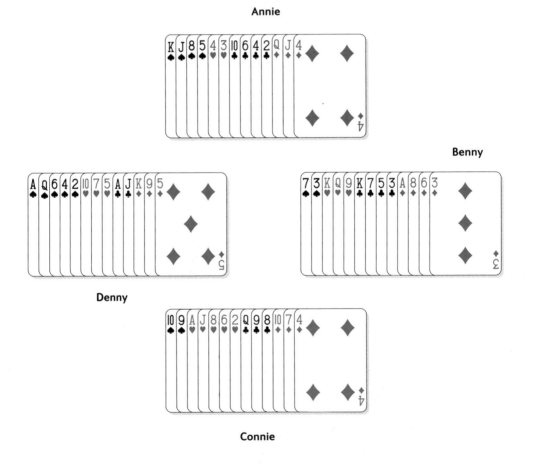

Above: *Annie thinks she will win three tricks, Benny four, Connie two, Denny five, so A-C want to make five tricks to B-D's nine. Annie leads* **2♣** *(by law). In play, Denny wins four tricks and everybody else three. So A-C bid five, won five plus an overtrick, score 51; B-D bid nine, won only seven, so lose 90 points.*

Play: To the first trick everyone must play their lowest Club. If you haven't any Clubs, you may play anything except a Spade. Follow normal Whist rules, except that you may not lead a Spade to a trick until someone has 'broken' the suit by trumping a trick started in a different suit (or, of course, unless you hold nothing but Spades).

Score: A side that takes at least as many tricks as its bid scores 10 times its bid, plus 1 per overtrick. There is a penalty, however, for consistent underbidding. When, over a series of deals, a side's overtricks total 10 or more (as witnessed by the final digit of their cumulative score), their score is reduced by 100, and any overtricks above 10 carried forward to the next cycle of 10. This is called sandbagging.

Example: A side has a score of 488, and on the next deal bid five and win nine tricks. This brings them to 538 plus 4 for overtricks, making 542. For the excess of 12 overtricks they deduct 100, bringing them to 442 and leaving them with an excess of 2 towards the next cycle.

For a failed contract, a side loses 10 points per trick bid.

For a successful nil bid, the nil-bidder's side scores 50 points, in addition to the score won (or lost) by their partner for tricks made. If it fails, the nil-bidder's side loses 50 points, but any tricks taken by the nil-bidder may be counted towards the fulfilment of their partner's contract. Blind nil scores on the same principle, but doubled to 100.

Game: The game is won by the first side to reach 500 points.

COLLUSION

A simple Whist variant for four players. In this fun game you keep making and breaking partnership agreements with other players.

❖ **Cards:** 52, as for Whist.

❖ **Deal:** The turn to deal passes to the left. Deal 13 cards to each player, face down, in ones.

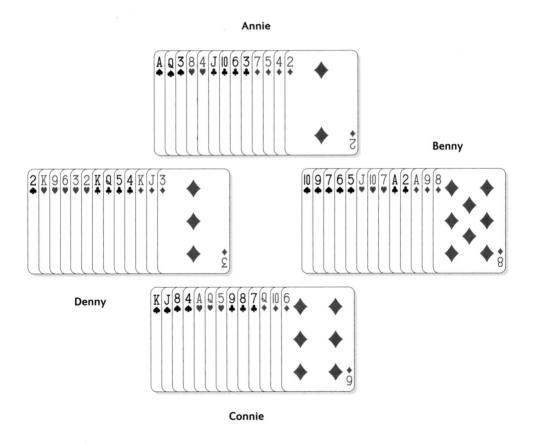

Above: Annie estimates that she will win two tricks, Benny four, and Connie 3. Denny, also thinking two, offers to partner Annie in a bid to win four between them. Connie revises hers to four, making a possible alliance with Benny.

❖ **Trumps:** None.

❖ **Object**: To win exactly the same number of tricks as one other player.

❖ **Play:** Follow normal Whist rules of trick play. The dealer's left-hand neighbour leads to the first trick.

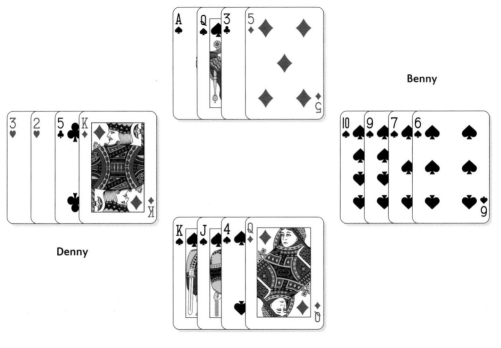

Annie

Benny

Denny

Connie

Above: *After nine tricks Annie has won none, Benny two, Connie three, Denny four, and these are the cards remaining, with Denny to lead. He asks Connie which suit she would like and she replies 'Spades would be nice', as she needs one more trick to match Denny's four. If successful, she and Denny would score 4 each plus a bonus of 10, giving them both 14 and ensuring that Annie and Benny can't match each other. Unfortunately, Denny has no Spade, so Connie says 'Diamonds, then'. More unfortunately for both, Denny's King takes the trick and he also wins the last three, since no one can follow suit to his Clubs or Hearts. Result: Annie 0, Benny 2, Connie 3, Denny 8. No two have won the same number, so Annie, with fewest, adds a bonus of 20 and scores that number of points.*

❖ **Score:** Each player scores 1 point per trick won. In addition:

- If two players win the same number of tricks, they each add a bonus of 10.

- If all four win a different number of tricks, whoever won fewest adds a bonus of 20.

- If three players win the same number of tricks, the fourth adds a bonus of 30.

❖ **Game:** Whoever first reaches 100 points wins the game. However, this total must include a bonus, and not be reached by scoring for tricks alone. If you exceed 99 without earning a bonus, you must deduct the number of tricks you took from your total instead of adding it.

❖ **Colluding:** The point of the game is that any two players may collude by arranging to win the same number of tricks as each other. For example, they may say 'I'm going for four', or 'I probably won't take any more', or may ask another player what suit to lead or avoid leading. All such agreements are informal, and alliances may be broken and re-formed in the light of subsequent events.

EUCHRE

The game for which the Joker was invented remains popular in many parts of the world, though played to various different rules. Here's the simplest version.

❖ **Players**: Two or three.

❖ **Cards**. 25, made by stripping numerals 2 to 8 and adding a Joker (or a **2♠**, called the 'Benny').

❖ **Rank of cards**: Cards rank downwards A K Q J 10 9 in non-trump suits. In trumps the order is:

1 Joker, or Best Bower (rhymes with 'flower')

2 Jack of trumps, or Right Bower

3 The other Jack of the same colour as trumps, or Left Bower

followed by Ace, King and so on. The trump suit is therefore one card longer, and the other suit of its colour one card shorter, than the other two plain suits.

❖ **Deal**: Deal five cards each in batches of three and two. Stack the rest face down; they aren't used.

✤ **Trumps:** Turn up the topmost of the undealt cards to show a preferred trump suit.

✤ **Object:** The 'maker' aims to win at least three of the five tricks played, ideally five.

✤ **Bidding:** Each in turn, starting with the dealer's left-hand neighbour, bids to become the maker by accepting the preferred suit as trump (saying 'I order it up'). If no one will, the card is turned down and each in turn may now offer a different suit as trump. If still no one will, the dealer must.

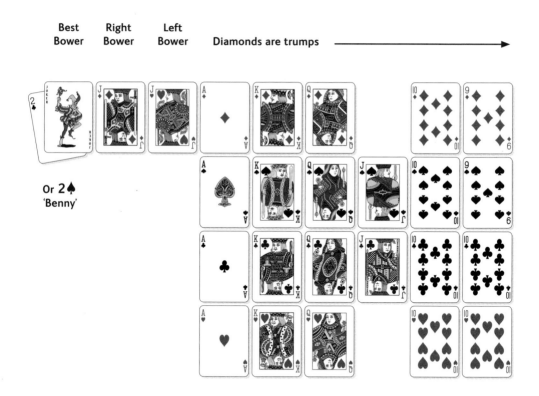

Best Bower	Right Bower	Left Bower	Diamonds are trumps ⟶

Or 2♠ 'Benny'

Above: The highest trump is the Joker (Best Bower) or **2♠** *(Benny). If Diamonds are trumps, the Right Bower (second highest) is the* **J♦** *and the Left (third highest) the* **J♥**, *followed by Ace etc. down to Nine. The other red suit, Hearts, is one card short because its Jack is the Left Bower.*

❖ **Taking the turn-up**: If the turned suit is ordered up, the dealer may exercise the privilege of taking it in exchange for any unwanted card (which is laid face down).

❖ **Play:** The dealer's left-hand neighbour leads to the first trick and the winner of each trick leads to the next. You must follow suit if you can, but may otherwise play any card. The trick is taken by the highest card of the suit led, or by the highest trump if any are played. Note that the bowers all belong to the trump suit. So if Diamonds are trumps, then Benny and **J ♥** are the first and third highest Hearts. They can be played to a Heart lead and, if led, Hearts must be followed.

❖ **Scoring**: Score 1 point for each trick won, or 2 for 'the march' (all five).

❖ **Game:** The winner is the first to reach 5 points, or any other agreed target.

FORTY-ONE

An interesting variety of Whist that is popular in Syria.

✤ **Players:** Four, sitting crossways in two partnerships of two.

✤ **Object:** Although each player scores alone, the winning side is the one in which one of its partners is first to reach a score of 41.

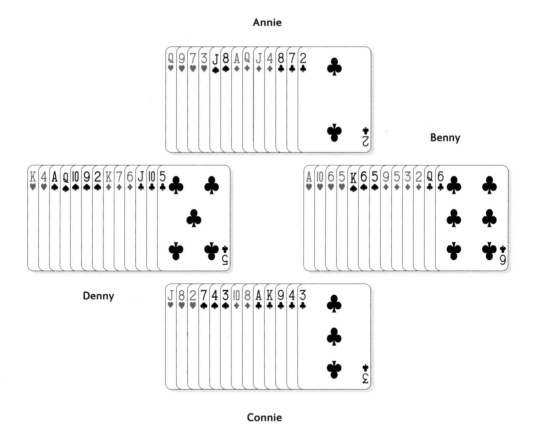

Above: In this deal Annie bid four but won only three tricks, Benny bid three but won two, Connie bid four and won five, Denny bid and won three. Annie scores -4, Benny -3, Connie +4, Denny +3.

Deal: Deal one card to each player, then 12 more, two at a time, till everyone has 13.

Trumps: Hearts are always trumps.

Bidding: Each in turn, starting with the dealer's left-hand neighbour, examines their cards and states the minimum number of tricks he or she expects to win. If the four bids total less than 11 the cards are thrown in and the deal passes on. But bids of seven or more count as double, so any such bid means that play will proceed.

Play: Follow normal rules of Whist play.

Score: Bids of 1 to 6 score, if successful, 1 point per trick bid (even if more were made). If unsuccessful, the bidder loses 1 point per trick bid. Bids of 7 or more count 2 as points per trick bid, won or lost.

Game: Scores are kept cumulatively and the first to reach 41 wins for his or her side.

NAP

Short for Napoleon, this simpler relative of Euchre is played, in one form or another, throughout Northern Europe.

❖ **Players:** Three to seven, best with four to five.

❖ **Cards:** 52 cards, but often reduced to 28 by omitting all numerals below 8.

❖ **Also needed**: Counters, poker chips or coins; at least 50 each.

❖ **Deal:** Deal five cards each, either in ones or as batches of 3+2.

❖ **Object:** To become the highest bidder and win at least three tricks.

Below: *Annie bids to win two tricks, thinking of Hearts as trumps and hoping to make both Kings. Benny bids three, which he can certainly make with Clubs as trumps. Connie's low cards prompt her to bid miz with a view to losing every trick. This will succeed, unless Benny raises his bid to four and hopes that upon leading a Spade to his fourth trick nobody will be able to follow suit.*

Benny

Annie

Connie

✤ **Bidding:** Starting with the dealer's left-hand neighbour, each in turn passes or bids to win a stated number of tricks. Each bid made must be higher than the previous one. A bid is an undertaking to win at least the number of tricks stated, using a trump suit of one's own choice. From low to high, the bids are:

- two tricks

- three tricks

- miz (lose every trick)

- four tricks

- Nap (five tricks)

- Wellington (five, for double stakes)

- Blücher (five, for redoubled stakes). Wellington may only follow a bid of Nap, and Blücher a bid of Wellington.

Play: The highest bidder leads to the first trick. The suit of the card led is automatically trump, except in miz, which is played at no trump.

You must follow suit if you can, but may otherwise play any card. The trick is taken by the highest card of the suit led, or by the highest trump if any are played, and the winner of each trick leads to the next.

Score: If successful, the bidder wins from each opponent 2 to 4 units for bids of two to four respectively, 3 for miz, 10 for Nap, 20 for Wellington and 40 for Blücher. If not, pay the same amount to each opponent, though it may be agreed to halve it in the case of Nap, Wellington, and Blücher.

Later deals: The turn to deal passes to the left, and cards are usually not shuffled till a bid of five has been won.

Game: Play as many deals as agreed in advance.

Optional Joker: Some players add a Joker as the highest trump – or, in miz, as the only trump.

KNAVES

A nice little penalty-trick game ideal for three players.

❖ **Players**: Three.

❖ **Cards**: 52.

❖ **Deal**: Deal 17 cards each and turn the last face up to show the trump suit.

❖ **Object**: To win tricks, but avoid those containing one or more Jacks.

❖ **Play**: The dealer's left-hand neighbour leads to the first trick and the winner of each trick leads to the next. Follow suit if possible, otherwise play any card. The trick is taken by the highest card of the suit led or by the highest trump if any are played.

❖ **Score**: At end of play you each score 1 point per trick won and deduct penalty points for each Jack taken as follows: of Spades 1, Clubs 2, Diamonds 3, Hearts 4.

❖ **Game**: The winner is the first to reach 20 points.

-1   -2   -3   -4

Above: Each knave (Jack) taken in a trick incurs the penalty shown.

PUT

Frankly, this is a disreputable old English tavern game that died out in Queen Victoria's reign. But it is surprisingly good fun if you don't take it seriously and don't play for money. 'Put' is short for 'I put it to you that my cards are better than yours and that we therefore play for the whole stake instead of just this point. But I could be bluffing.'

- **Players:** Two, adaptable for three or four.

- **Cards:** 52, as for Whist.

- **Deal:** Deal three cards each, in ones.

- **Trumps:** None.

- **Play:** The non-dealer leads first. There is no rule of following: you can play any card to a trick. The trick is taken by the highest card, regardless of suit. If tied, the trick is discarded. The winner of each trick, or the leader of a tied trick, leads to the next.

Yvonne

Zandy

Above: *Before leading, Yvonne says 'Put'. Zandy accepts, and plays his Ace to Yvonne's. The first trick is tied. Yvonne 'puts' again, hoping to either win with her Ten or to bluff Zandy into ceding the point. Zandy accepts, and matches Yvonne's Ten with his own. Another tie. But Zandy's Nine prevails, and he scores the point.*

Putting: Either player, when about to play a card, may instead call 'Put'. The other may then resign, in which case, the putter scores the point without further play. If the non-putter insists on playing it out, then whoever wins the point jumps to 5 and wins the game outright. Neither scores if the point is put and the result is a tie.

Score: Score 1 point for winning two tricks, or one trick to two ties. If all three are tied, or both win a trick and the third is tied (known as 'trick and tie'), neither player scores.

HEARTS

Hearts is one of the earliest and best known games in which your aim is not to win tricks but to avoid winning tricks containing penalty cards – in this case, Hearts and the Queen of Spades. It is also one of the most widely available games to play online or on a computer.

- **Players**: Three to six.

- **Cards**: 52, from high to low A K Q J 10 9 8 7 6 5 4 3 2. If three play, omit **2♣** so they divide evenly (17 each).

- **Deal**: Deal all the cards around one at a time. If five or six play, those with one extra card play two cards to the first trick.

- **Object**: To avoid winning tricks containing Hearts or **Q♠**. Or, if your hand is strong enough, to win all 14 penalty cards – this is called 'hitting the moon'.

- **Exchanging cards**: Before play, you each pass three cards face down to your left-hand neighbour and receive three from your right.

- **Play**: Whoever holds **2♣** (**3♣** if three play) leads it to the first trick. You must follow suit if you can, otherwise you may throw any card – except on the first trick, to which, if unable to follow, you may not throw a Heart or the **Q♠**. The trick is taken by the highest card of the suit led, and the winner of each trick leads to the next.

- **Leading Hearts**: You may not lead a Heart to a trick until Hearts have been 'broken' – that is, at least one player has already taken a heart – or unless your only alternative is to lead the **Q♠** (though you may lead her if you wish). Some say you may lead a Heart when **Q♠** has been played to a trick. Agree on this beforehand.

- **Score**: At end of play you each count 1 penalty point for each Heart you have taken in tricks, and 13 for **Q♠**.

✤ **Hitting the moon**: However, if you take all 14 penalty cards, you either deduct 26 points from your current score, or add 26 to everyone else's.

✤ **Game**: The winner is the player with fewest points when one or more players reach or exceed 100 points.

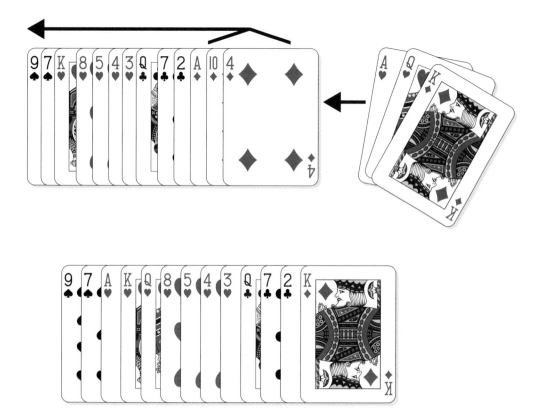

Above: In passing three cards to your left and receiving three from your right you keep the Spades as they will protect you in the event of your receiving **A, K** or **Q♠** . Your Hearts are almost certainly safe, the only danger being if somebody leads **2♥** when the others have no Hearts left. Pass on three Diamonds in hope of voiding that suit so that you can discard a high Heart when the first Diamond is led. In this example, the cards you get from your right-hand neighbour do not damage the hand.

HEARTS FOR TWO PLAYERS

❖ **Deal:** Deal 13 each and stack the rest face down as a draw pile. Upon winning a trick, you draw the top card of the draw pile, add it to your hand, wait for your opponent to draw the next, then lead to the next. Keep playing till all cards have been played out.

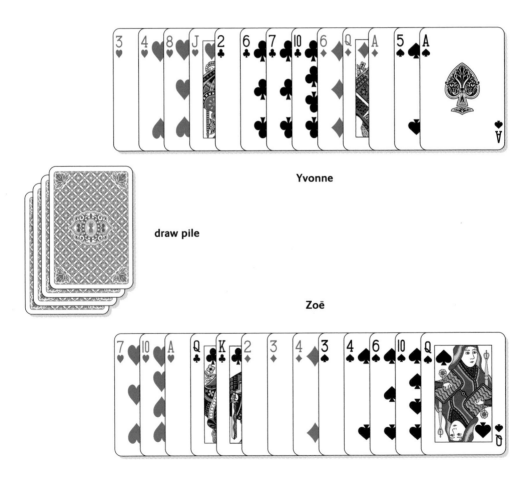

Yvonne

draw pile

Zoë

Above: *After each trick, the winner draws the top card and the loser the second.*

PARTNERSHIP HEARTS

Hearts for four players is best played in two partnerships of two each. Follow the rules for basic Hearts but with these differences.

❖ **Exchanging cards:** Before play, you each pass three cards face down to your left-hand neighbour and receive three from your right. On the second deal, pass three to your left and receive three from your right. On the third deal, exchange three with your partner. On the fourth there is no exchange. Repeat this pattern throughout.

❖ **Score:** Each partnership keeps its won tricks together and scores as if it were one player.

PARITY

This simple trick-taking game for two requires a deal of attention and concentration, as each knows exactly what cards the other holds.

❖ **Players:** Two.

❖ **Cards:** 30, consisting of A, K, Q, J, 10, 5, 2, in each suit plus two Jokers, one of each colour.

❖ **Card order:** The Jokers are always the two highest trumps, that of the trump colour being highest, followed by that of the other colour, followed by the Ace.

For example, if Hearts are trumps, the top card is the red Joker, second highest the black Joker, followed by A K Q J 10 5 2.

❖ **Deal:** Whoever cuts the lower card deals first and the turn to deal alternates. Shuffle thoroughly between deals and deal 15 cards each in ones.

❖ **Object:** To win either an even or an odd number of tricks, as specified before play.

❖ **Trumps:** You both examine your cards and the non-dealer nominates a trump suit.

❖ **Odd or even:** The dealer then specifies whether the aim is to win an odd or an even number of tricks.

✤ Play: The non-dealer leads to the first trick. You must follow suit if you can, but may play any card if you can't. The trick is taken by the higher card of the suit led, or by the higher trump if any are played, and the winner of each trick leads to the next.

✤ Score: Only the player who wins an appropriate number of tricks (odd or even as specified) scores. The score is 10 points for winning, plus 1 point for each trick won. If you win none, it counts as an even number. Thus the lowest possible score is 10 (target even, win 0 tricks) and the highest 25 (target odd, win all 15 tricks).

✤ Game: The first to reach a total of 100 points wins.

Yvonne

Zandy

Above: Zandy dealt. Yvonne chooses Clubs as trumps, the black Joker outranks the red. Zandy specifies the target number of tricks as odd. In fact, as anticipated, he wins two Club tricks, two Hearts, two Spades and one Diamond, giving him seven tricks and a score of 17.

CUCUMBER

> A northern European gambling game that needn't be taken too seriously, and can easily be scored in writing. Of many different versions of the game, the following is the simplest.

✤ **Players:** Three to seven.

✤ **Cards:** 52, running from high to low A K Q J 10 9 8 7 6 5 4 3 2.

✤ **Deal:** Deal six cards each, one at a time.

✤ **Object:** To avoid being left with the highest card after playing to five tricks.

✤ **Play:** The dealer's left-hand neighbour leads to the first trick. Each in turn must then play a card equal to or higher in value than the previous card played, regardless of suit. If you can't play an equal or higher card, you must play the lowest you have. Whoever plays the highest card, or was last to play the highest card, wins the trick. Tricks are not kept separate; in fact, it is usual simply to play each of your cards face up in front of you.

❖ **Score:** After the fifth trick, everyone reveals their last card. Whoever has the highest of them scores penalty points equal to its face value, counting Ace as 14, King 13, Queen 12, Jack 11, numerals as marked. If tied, both or all receive the same penalty points.

❖ **Continuation:** Upon reaching 21 penalty points you lose a life, but may start again with the same score as that of the player with the next highest score. Next time you reach 21, you are 'sliced' (like a cucumber) and drop out of play. When only two players remain, keep going till one of them is sliced. The winner is the player with the lowest accumulation of penalty points.

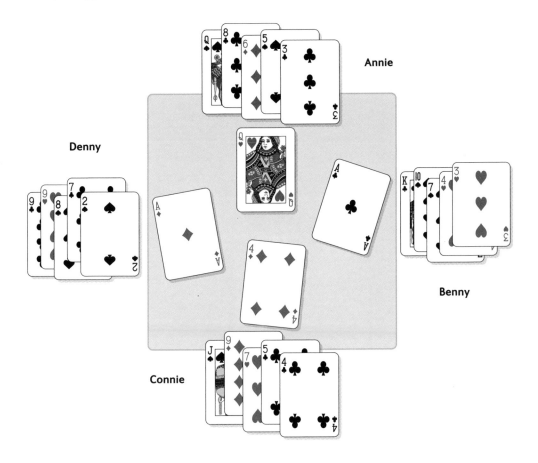

Above: *Annie leads* Q♥. *Benny overtakes, and now Connie must play her lowest card (either of her Fours). Denny doesn't want to be forced to play his Two, so wins with* A♦, *the last played of equally high cards. He will then lead a Nine.*

SEDMA

Sedma is the Czech for 'Seven'.

- **Players:** Four, in two partnerships of two each.

- **Cards:** 32, ranking A 10 K Q J 9 8 7 in each suit. (**Note:** Ten is second-highest.)

- **Deal:** Deal eight cards each in ones.

- **Object:** To win Aces and Tens in tricks and to win the last trick. Aces, Tens and the last trick score 10 points each, making 90 in all.

- **Partnerships:** A game is typically 12 deals. Partners are changed after every four deals, so that everyone partners everyone else an equal number of times and a single player wins.

- **Play:** Dealer's left-hand neighbour leads to the first trick, and the winner of each trick leads to the next. You needn't follow suit, but can always play any card you like. All Sevens are trumps. A trick is taken by the last played card of the same rank as the one led, or by the last played Seven if any are played.

Examples:

1. Played: 9 J A J. The Nine wins, having been neither matched nor trumped, and the trick counts as 10 for the Ace.

2. Played: 9 A A 9. The second Nine wins a trick worth 20.

3. Played: 9 7 J 10. The Seven trumps a trick worth 10.

4. Played: A 7 7 A. The second Seven wins a trick worth 20.

5. Played: 7 7 7 7. The last-played Seven wins.

Score: You each score the points made by your own partnership. These scores are carried forward, and the winner is the player with the highest total after 12 deals.

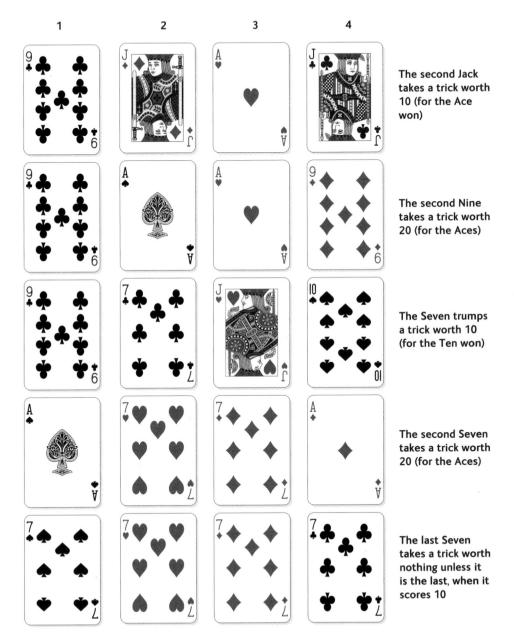

The second Jack takes a trick worth 10 (for the Ace won)

The second Nine takes a trick worth 20 (for the Aces)

The Seven trumps a trick worth 10 (for the Ten won)

The second Seven takes a trick worth 20 (for the Aces)

The last Seven takes a trick worth nothing unless it is the last, when it scores 10

Above: *How tricks are won. In these five examples the cards are played in the order shown (1, 2, 3, 4).*

For the most part these are a special class of collecting
and matching games, since the object is generally to
take cards at random from a shuffled pack and get them
back into order, typically into four suit-sequences of
13 cards each, by means of various procedures often
resulting in pretty patterns.

ONE-PLAYER GAMES

CRAZY QUILT

A traditional game, looking like patchwork and requiring a large table, unless you use miniature cards.

- **Cards:** 104 (two packs).

- **Layout:** Take one Ace and one King of each suit and place them aside as bases. Shuffle the rest and deal the next 64 into a square of eight rows and eight columns, arranging them alternately horizontally and vertically. This forms the 'quilt'.

- **Object:** To build on each Ace a 13-card suit-sequence up to its King, and on each King down to its Ace.

- **Play:** Hold the other 32 cards face down as a stock, turn them over one at a time, and play each one if you can or else discard it face up to a single waste pile.

- **Building cards:** You can build it on an Ace pile if it is the next highest card of the same suit, or on a King pile if the next lowest, or you can place it on a card of the quilt if it's the next highest or lowest, regardless of suit, though you must keep each packet going in the same direction once you're under way.

The top card of the waste pile is always available for either of these actions. So is the top card of any packet in the quilt, so long as at least one of its shorter edges is free.

For example, in the initial layout (*see* opposite) only the 16 cards projecting from the edges of the quilt can be used. You can also, if possible, transfer the top card of an Ace pile to the King pile of the same suit, if it fits, and vice versa.

‡ **Re-deal:** When you run out of stock cards, you may turn the waste pile once and deal through it again.

‡ **Success:** Quilt should come out more often than not.

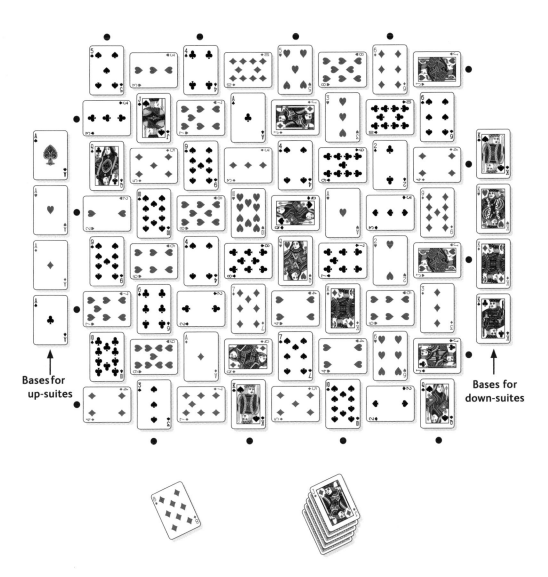

Above: *Cards with at least one short edge free (marked with a spot in this initial layout) are available for building on suits or packing on the waste pile. The 2♥ may be built immediately, enabling Q♠ to go on K♣.*

DEMON

A popular game throughout the English-speaking world, Demon is as hard to get out as its name implies.

❖ **Cards:** 52.

❖ **Layout:** Deal a packet of 13 cards face down and turn the top one face up. These form a reserve called the Demon. Deal the next card face up as the first of four base cards, then deal four more cards in a row beneath it to start the layout. Hold the remaining 45 face down as a stock pile.

❖ **Object:** As the three other cards of the same rank as the first base become available, move them up into a row next to it. Build on these upwards in suit and sequence till each contains 13 cards, the top card one rank lower than the base.

For example, if the base cards are Fives, each pile will run 5 6 7 8 9 10 J Q K A 2 3 4.

❖ **Play:** Turn cards from the stock in sweeps of three at a time and play them face up to a single waste pile. After each sweep, see if you can enter the top card of the waste pile into the game. It can go on one of the base piles if it's the next highest card of the same suit. Or it can go to the top of one of the layout cards if it's the next lowest card of the opposite colour (for example, 10♥ or 10♦ on J♠ or J♣).

❖ **Playing from the layout:** You can also play the top card of a layout pile to a base pile if it continues the suit sequence. Spread these layout piles into columns so you can identify each card. You may move either one card at a time or complete sequences from column to column, provided that the join follows the rule.

❖ **Playing from the Demon:** You can always play off the top card of the Demon if it fits the top of a base pile or a column in the layout. You then turn the card beneath it face up.

❖ **Emptying the layout:** Whenever you play the last card from a column, you must fill it at once with the top card of the Demon – or, if none remains, of the waste pile. You may not fill it from the pack or from elsewhere in the layout.

❖ **Re-deal**: Keep turning the waste pile and re-dealing until the game either blocks or comes out.

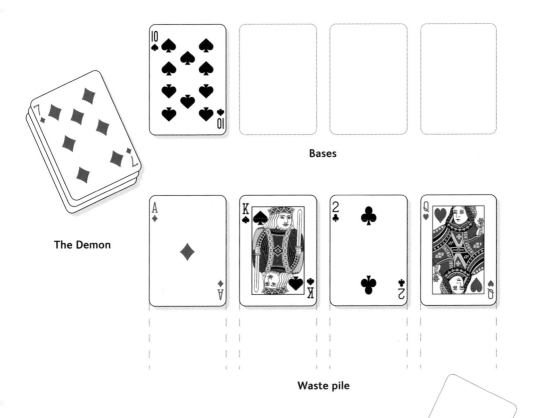

Bases

The Demon

Waste pile

Above: *In this example you must set the other Tens out as bases, as and when they appear, and build them all up in suit (via -Q-K-A-2-) to the Nines. Unusable cards go to the waste pile. The top card of the Demon and the waste pile are always available for building. Columns are to be built downwards in opposite colours. In this very improbable case, for example, you can start by playing* **A♦** *to* **2♣**, *then* **K♠** *to* **A♦**, *then* **Q♥** *to* **K♠**, *leaving three spaces, which you can fill with the top three cards of the Demon.*

QUADRILLE

An old but pretty little game representing a courtly dance.

❖ **Cards:** 52.

❖ **Layout:** Arrange the four Queens decoratively in the centre. Around them arrange the Fives and Sixes as base cards.

❖ **Object:** Build on each Six upwards in suit to the Jack (6 7 8 9 10 J), and on each Five downwards in suit to the King (5 4 3 2 A K).

❖ **Play:** Turn cards from the stock and build them if possible or discard them face up to a single waste pile if not.

❖ **Re-deal:** When you run out of cards turn the waste pile face down, without shuffling, and use it to continue as before.

❖ **Success rate:** You have a 50–50 chance of it working out.

Below: Turn cards from the stock (right) and play them if possible or else discard them to a waste pile. You can always use the top card of the waste pile if it fits on to a building pile.

Waste pile

Stock

KLONDIKE

This one is so well known that many just call it **Patience** or **Solitaire** without realizing that it has its own name.

 **Cards:** 52.

 **Deal:** Deal seven piles of cards in a row, face down, with one card in the first, two in the second, three in the third, and so on up to seven in the last. Then turn the top card of each pile face up.

Stock

Aces to be placed here and built up to Kings

Above: *You can make a good start by transferring 8♥ to 9♣, then 7♠ to 8♥, then 3♣ to 4♥. The space left by moving 7♠ can be filled with the top card of the stock.*

❖ **Object:** To put out the four Aces as and when they appear, and to build each one up in suit and sequence to the King.

❖ **Play:** Turn cards from the stock one by one and play them if possible or else discard them face up to a single waste pile.

❖ **Playing to the base piles:** Any available card can be placed on a base pile when it continues the sequence. Available cards are:

- The card you just turned from the stock

- The top card of the waste pile

- The top card of a column in the layout.

❖ **Managing the layout:** Spread the cards in the layout columns so all are visible. An available card that can't be played to a base pile can be played to the exposed end of a column, provided it's the next lowest rank and of opposite colour.

You can transfer any single exposed card, plus any cards in sequence visible below it, from one column to another, provided the join follows the descending-alternating rule.

Whenever you uncover a down card, turn it face up. Whenever you clear out a column, you may start a new one, but only with a King (plus any other cards that may be in sequence to it).

❖ **Re-deal:** None.

❖ **Note:** Some players turn cards from the stock in fans of three, of which only the uppermost (after turning) is available. If played it releases the one below, and so on. If it is unplayable, all three must be discarded to the waste pile in the same order. If this method is used, the waste pile may be turned twice, giving three rounds of play in all.

❖ **Success:** Klondike should come out more often than not.

GOLF

A long-popular game, so-called because all 52 cards are putted one by one on to a single pile representing a hole. The number unputted at the end of play is your handicap for the round.

❖ **Cards:** 52.

❖ **Deal:** Deal seven cards face up in a row to start the layout, then another seven in a row across the tops of them, and continue till you've dealt out 35 cards in five rows of seven. Deal the next card face up to the table, to represent the 'hole', and turn the remaining 16 cards face down as a stock.

❖ **Object:** To clear all the cards up by 'putting' them into a continuous pile on the 'hole'.

❖ **Play:** At each turn, putt the top card of one of the seven piles to the hole if it's one rank higher or lower than the existing hole card. For example, if the hole card is a Seven, you can putt either a Six or an Eight, regardless of suit. Aces and Kings are not consecutive: only a Two will go on an Ace, and only a Queen on a King.

Below: You can start by putting 7♠ on to 8♣, followed by 9♦, 10♠, then reverse direction with 9♥. No Eight or Ten is now available, so you turn the next card from the stock to get going again.

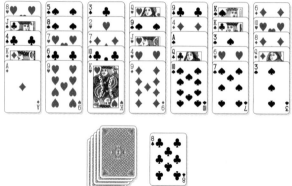

When stuck, turn the next card from the stock and putt, regardless of whether it continues the sequence, and continue play as before.

❖ **Re-deal:** None.

❖ **Success:** If you run out of stock before the layout piles are empty, you have lost.

BLACK HOLE

Similar to Golf, but all cards are visible to start with, so the game should always come out with careful play.

❖ **Cards:** 52.

❖ **Deal:** Place the **A♠** in the middle of the table to represent the black hole.

❖ **Object:** To clear all the cards off the layout by building them up into a continuous pile on the hole. This pile must consist of numerically consecutive cards either upwards or downwards, and changing direction as often as you like. So, for example, it might run A 2 3 2 A K Q J Q K A and so on.

❖ **Layout:** Deal the other 51 cards out face up in 17 'fans' of three each in an orbit round the black hole.

❖ **Play:** The top card of each fan is available for dumping into the hole, and the play of one releases the one below.

❖ **Success:** This one should always come out, provided you try not to change direction too often.

*Right: You can start by shifting into the black hole (**A♠**) either **2♦**, or **K♥** or **K♣**, and continue from there. This particular layout came out successfully by starting with **2♦** and continuing upwards throughout, without once changing direction.*

NAPOLEON AT ST HELENA

The popular legend that Napoleon played Patience when exiled on St Helena comes from a misunderstanding of a historical document. But that didn't stop succeeding generations of players inventing new games based on Patience. This one is also known as Forty Thieves.

- ❖ **Cards:** 104 (two packs).

- ❖ **Deal:** Deal 10 cards face up in a row, then 10 more face up across them, and so on until you have 10 piles of four. Spread them slightly into columns so that all are identifiable. Hold the remaining 12 face down as a stock.

- ❖ **Object:** To set the Aces out, as and when they become available, and build each one up in suit and sequence to its King.

Play: Turn cards from the stock one at a time and play them if possible or else discard them face up to a single waste pile.

Available cards: These are the top card of the stock, the top card of the waste pile, and the top card of each of the 10 layout piles. An available card may be used for starting a base pile sequence if it is an Ace, or for continuing a sequence built on an Ace if it fits.

Managing the layout: Alternatively, it may be placed on the top card of one of the layout piles if it is of the same suit and next lowest in rank. Only one such card may be moved at a time. When a column is emptied, you can fill its space with any available card. You don't have to fill it immediately; you may prefer to wait for a better one to become available.

Success: This one rarely comes out, but if you allow yourself to re-deal the waste pile it probably will eventually.

Stock   Waste pile   **Base piles for eight Aces – build them up in suit to the Kings**

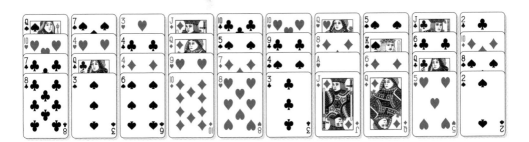

Above: Unfortunately, no Ace is immediately available for starting a base pile. However, you can shift the 10♦ to J♦ then both of them to the Q♦, thereby releasing A♥. You can also move 2♠ to 3♠. After that, you will have to start turning cards from the stock.

STRATEGY

A game of utmost simplicity, yet one that requires a great deal of care and forethought.

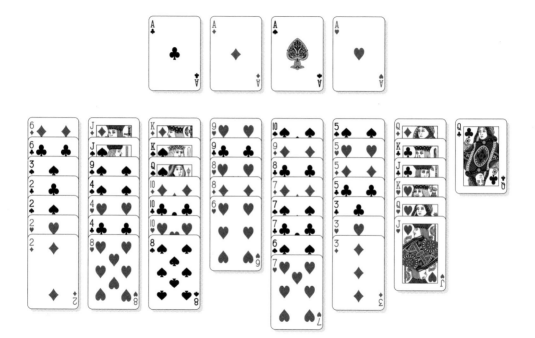

Above: *Place cards drawn one by one from the stock into any of eight waste piles, setting out the Aces as and when they appear, then build on the Aces upwards in suit to the Kings, taking only the bottom (exposed) card of a column at each turn. This one came out successfully – requiring only seven waste piles. The Q♣ could not have gone on the J♥ because it would have blocked the J♣. The real challenge is to create as few waste piles as possible. Even five has been done successfully. Note how helpful it is to place cards of the same rank on top of one another (like the four Twos and Fives), and descending sequences of the same suit (like the **K-Q-J♥**).*

Cards: 52.

Deal: None! Just hold the pack face down and play cards one by one from the top.

Object: To set out the Aces as they become available and build each one up in suit and sequence to its King.

Play: Turn cards from the stock and place each one face up to start or continue any of eight waste piles. As the table is empty to start with, the first card automatically starts the first waste pile. The next card you turn can either be placed on the first one, or used to start a second waste pile, and so on until you have a maximum of eight. Whenever you turn an Ace, do not play it to a waste pile but set it out as a base at the top of the table.

Managing the waste piles: You don't start building on any of the Aces till all 48 other cards have been played face up to the waste piles. The waste piles should be spread towards you in columns so that their contents are identifiable.

Building: Having dealt them all out skilfully and successfully, you now build up the four sequences on the Ace piles by taking at each turn only the exposed card at the end of a column. If during play you have carefully considered the best column for each card, and avoided putting any card in a column already containing one that will need to come out earlier, you should have no difficulty getting the game out.

Success: With accurate play, it should come out over 90 per cent of the time.

Note: You needn't play the first eight cards to different waste piles, but can delay starting a new pile for as long as you like. If successful, you can try reducing the number of piles to seven in the next game you play, or even six for more of a challenge. It can be done in as few as five.

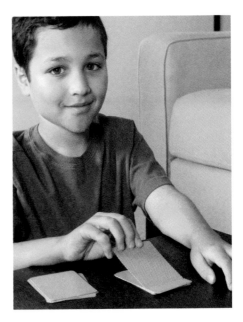

FREECELL

This modern adaptation of an old game called Eight Off started life as a freeware computer solitaire, and may have kick-started the whole new industry of online solitaires.

❖ **Cards**: 52.

❖ **Deal:** Deal eight cards face up in a row. Deal eight more across them, slightly overlapping so that the first cards remain identifiable. Deal four such rows, plus a fifth one of only four.

❖ **Cards:** Regard the result as eight columns, with seven in any of the first four and six in the others.

❖ **Object:** To release the Aces as and when they become available, set them up as bases above the columns, and to build each one up into a 13-card suit-sequence headed by the King.

Below: Three cards have been placed in the reserve in order to release three Aces, and the two red ones have been topped by their Twos. You might now continue by placing the **8♦** in the reserve to release **2♠**, or, better, putting it on the **9♣**, to be followed by **7♠**, **6♦**, **5♣**.

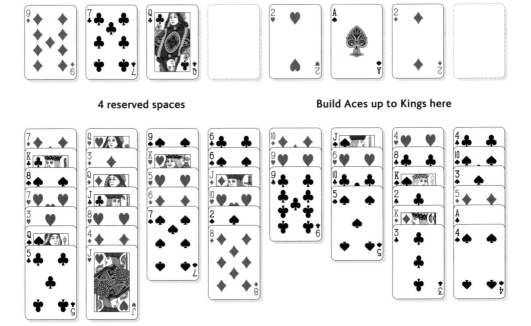

4 reserved spaces   **Build Aces up to Kings here**

❖ **Play:** The exposed card at the end of each column can be built on an Ace pile when it fits. Alternatively, you can pack it on the uncovered card at the end of another column in downward sequence and alternating colours. For example, a red Ten on a black Jack, a black Nine on the red Ten, and so on. You can move only one card at a time, not a packed sequence of two or more as a whole. When emptied, a column can be filled with any single available card to start a new one.

❖ **The reserve:** An available card may also be taken from the end of its column and set out by itself in a reserve. Up to four cards may be held in reserve at any time. Every card of the reserve is individually available for building on an Ace pile or packing on the end of a column whenever it fits.

❖ **Success:** With careful play, Freecell should come out most of the time.

ACCORDION

Accordion is more like a shedding game. It goes in and out, as you will see when you play it! (But without making a sound.)

Cards: 52.

Deal: None. Just hold the pack face down in one hand. With the other turn cards one at a time from the top.

Object: To finish up with a single pile of 52 cards in no particular order.

Play: Deal cards face up in a row from left to right. (If you're left-handed, reverse all left-right instructions.)

Whenever the card you turn matches the suit of the card on its immediate left, play it on top of the card it matches. Do the same if it matches the suit of the card last but one to the left.

Treat a pile of two or more cards as if it were just the one on top. Such a pile may never be split or separated.

Success: When you play the last card from hand you will, if you are very lucky, be able to make matching moves to the left until all 52 cards finish up in a single pile. Count half a win for finishing up with just two piles.

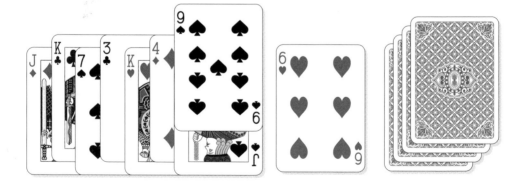

Above: *Dealing from left to right, the first few cards are not very helpful till you come to the* **9♠**, *which can be piled on the* **J♠** *(on its immediate left). This means that the next card you turn,* **6♥***, can go on the* **K♥***, which is now third on its left. And so on...*

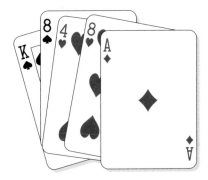

INDEX

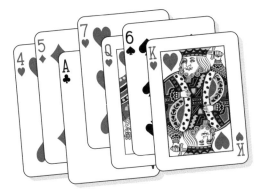

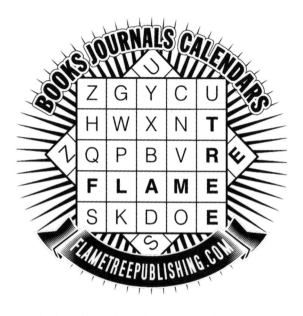

BOOKS JOURNALS CALENDARS

Z	G	Y	C	U
H	W	X	N	**T**
Q	P	B	V	**R**
F	**L**	**A**	**M**	**E**
S	K	D	O	E

FLAMETREEPUBLISHING.COM

SIGN UP FOR SPECIAL OFFERS